Studies in Social Policy and Welfare XXIII

ADOPTION, IDENTITY AND SOCIAL POLICY

The Search for Distant Relatives

Studies in Social Policy and Welfare

ADOPTION, IDENTITY AND SOCIAL POLICY

The Search for Distant Relatives

Erica Haimes and Noel Timms

Published by
Gower Publishing Company Limited,
Gower House,
Croft Road,
Aldershot,
Hants GU11 3HR,
England

Gower Publishing Company,
Old Post Road,
Brookfield,
Vermont 05036,
U.S.A.

British Library Cataloguing in Publication Data

Haimes, Erica
    Adoption, identity and social policy: the search for distant relatives.——(Studies in
    social policy and welfare)
    1. Adoption——England
    I. Title   II. Timms, Noel   III. Series
    362.7'34   HV875.7.G7
    ISBN 0-566-00888-2 (cased)
           0-566-00889-0 (paper)

Typeset by Vigo Press Ltd, Penge, London SE20
Printed in Great Britain by Biddles Ltd, Guildford, Surrey

Contents

Acknowledgements

The authors would like to acknowledge the help, advice and encouragement of the following: Peter Selman, Alf Davey, Tony Hall, Jane Aldgate, Jasmine Shell, Marie Johnson, Rita Timms and Robin Williams.

We would of course also like to thank all the adopted adults and social workers who provided much of the material upon which this book is based.

E. V. Haimes
N. W. Timms

1 Introduction

The significance of background

The research on which this book is based was conducted over a three-year period from 1980. It investigated the origins and working of one section (Section 26) of a complex piece of social legislation, the Children Act 1975. The particular provision in which we were interested concerned the compulsory counselling of a certain group of 'clients', namely those who had been adopted before the passing of the Act. This single provision carried a significance, historical and contemporary, far wider than would superficially be assumed. In an important sense it could be said to have 'made history'. It contained the first statutory reference to counselling, though the counselling appeared to be of a rather strange kind – compulsory. It carried retrospective force, in so far as it was interpreted as acknowledging some kind of breach of undertaking made between adoption workers and natural mothers in the past that it would be impossible for an adopted child to learn the identity of, and to make contact with, his or her natural parents. It was also about the making of personal history in the case of adopted people.

Our research was planned in two stages. First, we surveyed by postal questionnaire all local authorities, enquiring about the ways in which they had set about the implementation of Section 26 and their current procedures and organisation. Second, we undertook intensive interviewing of a selection of counsellors and applicants, so that we could appreciate the significance of the service for both sets of social actors and the problems each encountered. The combined results of the extensive and intensive phases, together with our historical study of the origins and early implementation of Section 26, enable us to understand an important piece of social legislation which had great personal significance. They also help us to use such understanding to illuminate the personal and social experience of adoption our society has organised.

The 'Distant Relatives' of our title refer to a particular kind of relations: those who are the natural parents and natural brothers and sisters of adopted people. However, conjecture about relatives, rendered distant by the passage of time, is common, in our society at least. Curiosity about family history is readily understandable; it is by no means curious. In some cases the curiosity will take an insubstantial form, a more or less idle fancy, seldom recurring. In other cases an interest may develop which is informed by something more than an expectation of tracing a clear link with the famous or the infamous, or even with seeing how far linear connections can reach. A preliminary understanding of such experiences, fitful or sustained, requires at least some reference to personal identity. People are interested in the past of their own relatives because this helps them to enlarge or deepen their knowledge of what is often called family or personal background. Aspects of identity will be discussed later in this book, but at this point it is important to note one implication of the place of 'background' in the notion we have of identity. Answering the question 'Who am I?', seems to require some reference to 'background'. It is insufficient to answer the question with the simple, foreground information conveyed by a name or by identifying oneself as the child of X, or by offering any equivalent equation. These pieces of information undoubtedly form part of the answer, but they do not constitute in themselves a fully satisfying response. The answer to the question 'Who am I?' must include some reference to the *kind* of person I am, and knowledge of background constitutes an essential ingredient to that judgement.

Lack of knowledge of background

For one particular group in our society lack of knowledge of background may be difficult to remedy, and its importance for the relevant social actors thereby increased. Adopted people are those whom complex legal decisions and psycho-social processes have changed from bearers of a potential history as the natural child of X to bearers of another history as the child of adoptive parents. The effect of adoption is that a person born of one union, of whatever duration or status, is treated legally as born of another. His or her relatives at the time of birth are from the point of adoption made distant by those processes and are often kept distant through the interactions of adopters and adopted people. And yet the background and the circumstances of conception and birth continue to be of crucial significance in the present. One of the adoptees we interviewed put it in starkly simple terms: 'You want to know if you are a child of love or lust.' It is important to note the tense used in this sentence: if you *are* a child of love or lust.

Yet, secrecy has been one of the key elements in adoption since it was first legally constituted in 1926. It has, of course, for some time been part of good adoption practice that a child should not be kept in ignorance of his or her adoptive status and should be told of the fact of adoption from an early age. However, even brief reflection on a more common subject of parental telling, namely telling children 'the facts of life', suggests how easily things may go wrong. In some families it might appear that the child is 'told' almost nothing else, whilst in others parents and sometimes children are quietly and continuously relieved that 'now' is not the time. Again, differences can easily arise over what information is being conveyed, and it may be difficult or impossible to refer to such difficulties even when they are apparent to one party or to both. As we shall see when we report on adopted people's experiences of 'being told' or 'having always known' about the adoptive status, 'telling' involves complex inter-actions over time.

Before 1975 adopted people in England and Wales (assuming that they knew they were adopted) were almost totally dependent on adopters for any information about their background. Some adoptive parents refused to reveal the fact of adoption, and the only documented source of information easily available to the adoptee was the adoption certificate. The existence of this, of course, would confirm any suspicions they had about being adopted, but would do little to satisfy even curiosity, since it only contains the person's adoptive name, date of birth, and the date and place of adoption. This certificate would be used in all situations which required a normal, long, birth certificate. With the introduction in 1947 of the short birth certificate (for use by adoptees and non-adoptees alike, instead of the long birth certificate) which did not mention adoption it could be the case that no documentary evidence of adoption was available to the adoptee at all. If, however, adopted people knew their original name and date of birth they could apply for their original long birth certificate and thereby acquire some information about their background, namely the natural mother's name, occupa-tion and address at the time of birth and possibly the natural father's name and occupation. Few adoptees realised that information could be acquired this way. Some, knowing they were adopted and wishing for this information, applied to the court to obtain an order requiring the Registrar General to supply the information, but applications were rarely granted. In Scotland, however, ever since the legal introduction of adoption in 1930, it was possible for an adopted person, on reaching the age of 17, to apply for the original birth certificate direct from the Registrar General, without using any

intermediary such as a court. What Section 26 of the 1975 Children
Act did was to make access to the original birth certificate almost as
easy in England and Wales as it already was in Scotland.

Section 26 attempted to manage both information as of right and
the agreed importance of safeguarding, as far as possible, the
interests of the three commonly identified 'parties' in adoption, the
child, natural parents and adoptive parents. Certain information
was now to be of right once an adopted person had attained the age
of 18, and it could be made available through public sources,
provided, in the case of those adopted before the passage of the Act,
the applicant 'attended an interview with a counsellor'. The
procedure devised to carry out the intention of Section 26 is
relatively complex and at an early stage in this book we think it
advisable to set it out in the form of a flow chart so that readers can
see the various stages and are able to refer back to illuminate any
later references in the text. The complexity of procedure reflects the
importance of the issue and the difficulties in any final reconciliation
of the interests of adoptee, adopters, natural parents and 'society':
the counsellor and the counselling are intended to contain, if not to
resolve such difficulties.

Application procedure for Section 26

1. Adopted person with a number of possible questions decides
   they may be answered by finding out, to a greater or lesser
   extent, about their origins

   ↓

2. Discovers General Register Office (Fareham) address from
   various possible sources.

   ↓

   Writes to Fareham.

   ↓

3. Receives application form from Fareham, asking for fairly
   basic information from the applicant; form asks where
   applicant wishes to be counselled. Fareham also send leaflet
   explaining the procedure.

   ↓

4. Fareham use this information to trace original records from
   Adopted Children Register.

5. Fareham send this inform-   6. Fareham inform applicant
   ation to wherever applicant   where the papers have been
   has chosen for counselling.   sent.

7. Counselling arranged and applicant is given the following information:
   (i) original name;
   (ii) natural mother's (and possibly father's) name;
   (iii) name of court which made adoption order;
   (iv) application form for original birth certificate;
   (v) authorisation to apply to court for name of placing agency.

8. Applicants who apply for birth certificate, find out:
   (i) date and place of birth;
   (ii) natural mother's (and possibly father's) name;
   (iii) natural mother's occupation;
   (iv) mother's address at time of birth;
   (v) name and address of person registering birth;
   (vi) date of registration;
   (vii) name of registrar.

9. Counsellor informs General Register Office (Fareham) that counselling has taken place and what he thinks the applicant intends to do.

So far we have introduced quite generally a subject of particular significance for adopted people: knowledge of origins and backgrounds. We have also outlined the procedures established under one section of a relatively new Act of Parliament which might be used by adopted people in their search for information. It is important to ground our study in both the general consideration of adoption and also in the detail which gives concrete meaning to the experience of being adopted, but the exposition so far perhaps runs the risk of losing sight of the individual adoptee. At this point, then, we hope to make more vivid the rather abstract notions of identity and background and the somewhat dry detail of administrative procedure by means of a case example taken from one of our interviews with 45 adopted people who had used Section 26. The use made of Section 26 by this particular applicant is not extensive but our summary of the research interview illustrates some of the main elements in discovery and search by adopted people.

A case example: Mrs A.
Mrs A. discovered she had been adopted when she was tracing the man she thought was her 'real' father. Her parents had divorced

when she was eight years old and she had subsequently lost touch with her father for about 30 years. Her interest in regaining contact was stimulated through a family tree project her son had been given at school, and her mother's death freed her to start enquiries.

> I found my father very easily and I got in touch with him and it just came out in conversation that I was an adopted daughter, I just hadn't any idea. I was absolutely stunned . . . and I must have been standing there I don't know how long, because the next thing I knew the dog was licking my hand . . . and I went back to work and people said, 'Oh, you do look pale,' and then I was all right. I wasn't upset, but I was shocked. I was just like a zombie the rest of the day; I was doing my work and my mind . . . the things that were going over and over in my mind, but it answered a few questions.

Mrs A. had for a long time felt that in appearance she was totally different from her family and that her consuming interests in life had 'never stemmed from my environment at all'.

Her first action after she had absorbed the news was to phone her relatives 'and they all knew and I thought this is why I think you should know, it's like finding your husband is going out with another woman, everybody knows except you.' She could understand why her adoptive mother had not told her – 'I must have been all she had left when they split up, and all she had left for the rest of her life' – but the others 'had known and never told me and no one's ever mentioned it. One or two thought I knew – and all my aunts kept saying, "Oh, but you were a lovely baby." That's not the point. What do you know, what can you tell me? None of them could tell me anything.'

Some information was forthcoming. Her adoptive father, whom she visited with her son ('I always thought I'd like to take them to see where I was a child'), 'remembered that my real mother looked after me for a long time'. A lady who had lived with them in the war recalled that

> my adoptive mum had me all the week and my real mother used to come and take me out at weekends, and after about so many months my mum said to my real mother, 'We're getting too fond of her and you've got to make your mind up whether you're going to give her up.' . . . So I think my mum – my real mother – was pressured . . .

The official start of Mrs A.'s search dated from the time she approached the local Registrar to ask about finding birth certificates. The Registrar told her about Section 26 and contacted Fareham on her behalf. She was informed that she had to have an interview 'with somebody from the Adoption Council'. The 'adoption counsellor' gave her 'this birth certificate and she said "You're going to be disappointed because there's no way you're going to or it's highly unlikely that you're going to be able to trace her because it was a private adoption, it wasn't through a society." And she said, "All I can suggest is a box number in a local paper." '

A few days later Mrs A. read an article about the Salvation Army's Missing Persons Bureau. She telephoned them and was told that the Salvation Army was not allowed 'to do adoptions'. The man she spoke to was very kind and very nice. Mrs A. then used the reference library to discover the origin of her unusual Christian names, and her adoptive father traced the address of the people for whom her natural mother had been working. Mrs A. wrote to them and was invited to visit.

They made such a fuss of me, like I was their long lost daughter. . . . They found out she [my mother] was pregnant while she was working for them and they didn't mind at all, let her stay on as long as she looked after their little girl. So she had the baby, went back to them, and stayed there another 14 months and then she went back to London. She was on her own, just a young girl on her own, no family, I found out since, so she could not keep me.

Mrs A. at this time saw herself as 'building up a picture of her mother', but getting no nearer. She contacted the Salvation Army again and went to spend a few days in London at St Catherine's House. She started, with her husband, trying to trace her mother's birth certificate, but an official responded to her approach by suggesting they use the record of marriages, since they knew her mother's maiden name. 'I just saw this name in print and I said to my son, "Look, that's my mother." It meant so much to me . . . this was my blood mother sort of thing, and it was an emotional thing.' She also traced a reference to her half-brother and discovered, because of his unusual surname, what seemed a likely address. At this point she again phoned the Salvation Army who advised caution and the use of an intermediary. Mrs A. decided to use the aunt in Scotland she had contacted as soon as she was told she was adopted.

The aunt phoned the half-brother and was given Mrs A.'s natural mother's phone number. 'So there we were, we'd got my mother and her phone number and my heart was pounding, my stomach was turning over . . .' The aunt then phoned Mrs A.'s natural mother who said she could not recall looking after a little girl called by Mrs A.'s Christian names. This seemed an insuperable barrier to the search, but Mrs A. wrote to her mother enclosing a snapshot of herself and her children.

> I said, 'I don't want in any way to interfere with your life, cause you any embarrassment or any upset' . . . how I'd had a happy childhood with no trouble there; I didn't want anything from her, I said, but you, your son and daughter, besides my own children are my only blood relatives, and I just want to meet you once, if only once . . .

She did not post this letter but took it to her mother's house and asked a neighbour to deliver it when she discovered her mother was not at home. The aunt then phoned Mrs A.'s mother again and the mother invited them to visit her.

'So we went the next day and she was lovely, and it was just the likeness . . . I am so like her.' Mrs A.'s mother had been hoping that her daughter would persist in her search and had regretted her earlier denial. She was concerned that her divorced husband might get to know of her past, but was fairly soon able to tell her grown-up children. 'I've met my half-brother and he was struck by the resemblance between my mother and me.' Mrs A. had always wanted brothers and sisters so discovering she had half-siblings was 'fantastic'. She learned from her mother that her father had not known of the pregnancy and she began to entertain some notions of trying to trace him:

> It's this genes thing that fascinates me and always has done, you know, in history and everything, things that you inherit; so I'd love to see photographs of him and his family and know what they do and what their interests are, that would satisfy me, but I don't suppose I ever will.

Mrs A. believed that she obtained two things from the Section 26 counsellor: mother's name ('I had this name . . . and I thought that is my mother – real mother, and before I had that, you see, you know all sorts of things go through your mind, whether she was somebody grand or somebody poor . . .') and the suggestion that she ought to consider her husband's possible feelings if they were to discover that her mother was in need. Mrs A. considered that the counsellor's 'main point that she was trying to get across to me was that I would most likely be disappointed.' The counsellor was 'very nice, very friendly. . . . I found her very encouraging but very matter-of-fact . . .' Mrs A. supported the law – 'it's essential that you have access to your own identity' – and thought that counselling was essential in the case of 'somebody young who's just found out and is impetuous.' She contacted the Salvation Army again rather than the counsellor: 'I felt she was just doing the job she had to do, which I thought she did very well.' She also believed, particularly in the early stages of the search, that she had to proceed warily.

Approach of this book

As we have just seen, Mrs A. learned of her adoption quite late in life, but the information of her status helped her towards a retrospective re-ordering of certain important items of self-knowledge. Her sense of difference from her adoptive family becomes a piece in a different jigsaw. She also interpreted the new information as imposing certain tasks: for example, she had to understand the actions of both her adoptive and 'blood' mother. It is within this context of the significance of knowledge that the part played by various officials (Registrars, Salvation Army, Section 26 counsellor) and by others should be understood. Mrs A.'s description of finding her natural mother's name and of her eventual contact with her and her half-brother clearly illustrates the importance of 'background' for adopted people. Her case suggests that access to birth information cannot easily be seen as an optional extra, and the task of Section 26 counsellors in relation to such information appears more than a simple administrative task. As we review these potentialities we see Section 26 against both the background of the history of adoption and against broader issues of identity in our society.

The way in which we can discern from the particular case of Mrs A. more general themes may be taken as a miniature of our overall approach to the presentation of the results of our study: to treat its various aspects within appropriately wider contexts. So, in the next chapter we discuss the origins of Section 26 in relation to changing ideas about the nature of adoption. Tracing the origins of Section 26 in earlier committee reports and in parliamentary debate shows how adoption and adopted people are defined and treated in a wider social context. Chapter 2 studies the implementation of Section 26. This sheds light on the way in which administrators, in central and in local government, treat adoption and on the path taken as one particular innovation in social policy is carried through to the point of action by the practitioners.

In Chapters 3 and 4 we examine the viewpoint of the practitioners and the problems they encounter in delivering Section 26 counselling. How they operate the service and the ways in which they define and solve their professional problems help us to see the ways in which the social organisation of adoption is maintained and managed. We are also given some understanding of social work itself. Not all the social workers acting as counsellors believe that Section 26 should have been enacted, and many found that the provision contained significant ambiguities which resulted in severe problems for practice. As one of them put it, 'It's like negotiating a new minefield.' Yet all were agreed that whatever Section 26 counselling meant it was without doubt a social work task. As they gave reasons why it was not appropriate work for other occupations and as they discussed problems and solutions, they allowed at least glimpses of the meaning of social work. In questions of definition the social workers we interviewed were almost totally uninterested. For them the meaning of social work (in the sense of its significance to themselves and to others) simply consisted in getting on with the task in hand in a way that was appropriate. In this it could not be said that our Section 26 counsellors were atypical, but exploring the point of their comments in the light of a new service helps to increase knowledge of social work as practice.

Practitioners are, of course, only one set of social actors in the provision we are considering. It is not only legislators, administrators and practitioners who make adoption what it is. So, Chapter 5 considers the perspective of users of Section 26 – the applicants, as we call them, or the 'clients' as sometimes they are inadvertently called. This chapter reports on their perceptions and appreciations of the work of Section 26 counsellors. It also aims to move beyond this to a consideration not simply of what they report but also of how they talk of the adoption experience and of Section 26. Abrams (1977), in an important review of the conceptual and practical problems of informal social care, suggested that the significance of the consumer/user perspective has still fully to be realised. We would argue that this situation arises because such a perspective is usually studied through simple, rather naive attention to consumer reports, treated as so much survey material. Closer attention to the talk of consumers and to how consumers talk of particular services reveals much more significant material.

Finally, in the three concluding chapters, we address directly the major themes that are interwoven with the substantive findings of earlier chapters. We seek an increased understanding of the adoptive experience through consideration of social – as contrasted with ego – identity. In this a narrative sense of self gains importance, and 'filling the gaps' in one's ignorance of the past achieves particular significance. The gaps are not discrete vacua to be filled with discrete pieces of information. Response to the 'failure' of society to provide information is also important, since it raises for adoptees and others significant questions concerning not simply the unavailability of such information but also the grounds on which it was not made available.

In the last chapter we link our social explanation of adoption and of social identity with issues outside the field of adoption, that is, child care generally conceived and also outside the field of general child care. The questions of social identity against which adoption practice might be measured arise in relation to other services, and strictly, indeed, to no social service at all. Children are in public care, away from their natural parents, for long periods; families are reconstituted through divorce, separation, etc.; families are constituted through such social (i.e. publicly sanctioned) procedures as artificial insemination by donor (AID). Has not social identity, as requirement and as social cause, a part to play in discussion of such questions?

A summary of the significance of our study would take the following form: our research concerns people who are at the edge of certain social boundaries, who may treat themselves and be treated by others as marginal in certain respects. It is not surprising that our results move across boundaries. Studying a provision which is seen as playing some part in the identity formation of individuals sheds some light on the identity of social work. A law which at least some social workers consider 'made history' in its retrospective undoing of previous 'promises' turns around the complex ways in which history-making is crucial for individuals. Studying an Act concerned at least in part with safeguarding the interests of traditionally identified parties in the adoption triangle (child, natural parent, adoptive parent) shows the importance of placing adoption in a much wider social context. As we learn of the adopted persons' attempts to place themselves in a social universe, we begin to see how the adoptive experience concerns society and how the experience of being adopted may be socially placed.

2 An innovation in adoption policy: origins and implementations

This book concerns the relationship between social identity and certain aspects of social policy. We attempt to reach this through a study of social actors at different levels – those of parliament, the national professional experts, the central and the local administrator, the practitioner and the user. These social actors are viewed as pursuing distinct but interrelated tasks – those of criticising, developing, devising and implementing – which together constitute the social organisation of adoption. These social actors and these social purposes are not viewed as so much scaffolding, dispensable once the grand theme of social identity is inscribed. Rather they form part of the social, changing form we in our society call adoption. The 1975 Act established through Section 26 a new principle, the right to access to certain birth information; and created a new service, counselling, characterised in a particular way to meet the special requirements of the time (i.e. it was compulsory). In order to explain how this came about (the sort of compromise it was) we examine the 'background' to the 1975 legislation. This chapter outlines the situation in relation to birth information as it was before the Houghton Committee on Adoption was appointed in 1969; the recommendations of the Committee are discussed and relevant issues in the debates leading to the Children Act are analysed; finally we consider briefly how the organisation for Section 26 counselling was established.

Birth information before Houghton

Legal adoption began as a service to childless couples as much as to homeless children. For the children it was seen as an opportunity for a 'fresh start'. So, many adoptive parents thought it best to make little or no reference to the fact of adoption through fear of stirring the child's curiosity about the past, or unsettling new and developing relationships. The power to 'change the name' of the adopted child, which became an almost automatic element in the proceedings, was also interpreted as serving the interests of natural parents, especially mothers, suffering the stigma of an illegitimate child. Their situation of 'having to forget' would, it was thought, be eased if all possibility of future contact between them and their child was removed. Should adopted people be curious, they had to contend not only with the possibility of a secretive attitude by the adoptive parents but also with a form of institutional secrecy: the information linking the adoption certificate with the original birth certificate was kept in a special register by the Registrar General and could only be revealed on approval of the courts. Such approval was very rarely given.

Further protection for adopters was provided through the 1949 Act which allowed them in all adoption applications to remain anonymous during the court proceedings. Consequently, their identity would not be known to the natural parents, and so any future attempts the latter might make to contact the child were effectively precluded. Adopters were also able to hide the fact of the adoption, since very few people would know their identity, and so they could take the 'fresh start' idea to its logical conclusion by pretending that the child was actually theirs.

The general opinion favouring concealment was reiterated in the consolidating 1950 Adoption Act. The notes relating to the sections on registration of births and adoptions state: 'the substitution . . . of the original birth certificate is considered desirable where that certificate revealed the fact of illegitimacy or where it is desired to conceal the origin of the child.' The appropriateness or otherwise of wishing to conceal a child's origins is not discussed. This perhaps implies that to do so was accepted practice. Circumstances were envisaged in which it might be necessary to know an adopted person's origins but, as in Scotland, these were limited to matters of inheritance: 'it will be impossible in ordinary circumstances for anyone to trace the origin and original birth certificate of an adopted child. In exceptional circumstances where for instance succession to property or title may be involved, the Registrar General will be able to supply the necessary information to persons entitled to it.'[1] No definition is given of entitlement, nor any explanation for the criteria by which the Registrar General would judge 'exceptional circumstances'. There is no indication that these circumstances would include anything like the applicant's need to know about natural background.

Opinion that adopted people might need birth information and that they may even be entitled to it was, however, beginning to form in professional circles. The Hurst Report states, 'A number of witnesses in England thought that the adopted person has a right to this information and expressed the view that it is not in the interests of adopted children to be permanently precluded from satisfying their natural curiosity.'[2] This appears to be the first official recognition of a number of facets of a slowly recognised problem: adopted people did develop curiosity about their backgrounds; such curiosity was not to be taken as a symptom of neurosis but as perfectly natural; there were, accordingly, benefits from providing this information; these benefits had to do with the person's psychological well-being, 'curiosity' and *needs*, as opposed to material interest in inheritance. For the first time also it was asserted that an adopted person had a 'right to this information'. Having acknowledged these factors, the Committee recommended that the age in Scotland before an adoptee could apply for information be raised to 21, but that this system should not be extended to England and Wales because of 'practical difficulties'. There was no explanation for this phrase. It was also recommended that adoptees in England, Wales and Scotland, when 21 years old, should be able to apply to the courts for a full copy of their adoption order. This would provide them with their original names and the names of their natural parents, and so give them sufficient information to obtain their original birth certificate in the ordinary way. There was no suggestion that 'exceptional circumstances' were necessary before such information would be supplied. For the first time the 'danger' of releasing this information was explicitly mentioned, only to be dismissed as 'slight'. This was seen as the possibility that natural mothers may be at risk of 'embarrassment' if traced by a child they had placed for adoption. It was also thought that most adoptees would be satisfied with information, rather than want to trace parents.

This was clearly a radical departure from all previous discussions on the matter and was the first attempt to break down institutional secrecy, rather than increase it. Such was the emphasis on the adopted person's welfare that natural parents' worries were dismissed and those of adoptive parents were never even mentioned. There was, however, no full debate on the Hurst Report in parliament, and the 1958 Adoption Act, which was based on the Report, maintained the *status quo:* information regarding an adopted person's origins would only be made available on application to a court and with proof of exceptional circumstances. The legislation also failed to include the Committee's recommendation that the application to adopt should include a pledge to tell the child of the adoption, though it accepted the suggestion that an explanatory memorandum be given to all adopters, stressing the need to tell the child. It is worth noting the content of the memorandum: 'You may prefer not to tell him anything; but that would be unwise, because he would be likely to find out himself sooner or later and if you had not told him, the discovery might be a shock.'[3] This 'shock' is almost a stronger form of the 'embarrassment' attributed to natural mothers: it contains no reference to either the process or the significance of discovery.

Houghton and the issue of birth information

The Houghton Committee, which began its work in July 1969, came to see access to birth information as a complex issue in itself and also one that touched on other aspects of adoption law. At its second meeting, in October 1969, it considered research projects then current. One of these, by John Triseliotis of Edinburgh University, concerned Scottish adoptees applying for birth records. The Committee viewed this positively, wondering how similar kinds of information might be obtained for England and Wales. They decided that invitations to organisations to submit further evidence would include questions on their experiences with any adoptees who were trying to trace their origins. Since it was intended to compile a Working Paper based on the evidence, individuals such as Triseliotis, and even some of the adoptees he had interviewed, could be invited to give further oral evidence. The Committee agreed that 'this was not a major issue',[4] but they did recognise that it reflected the changing nature of adoption: allowing access would weaken ideas of severance and of adoption as a 'fresh start'.

The evidence submitted in response to the invitation of November 1969 was marginally in favour of giving the adopted person as full information as possible, including natural parents' names. One organisation clearly in favour of such a move was, perhaps surprisingly, the National Council for the Unmarried Mother and her Child, which also argued against any court discretion in the matter. This organisation, using material partly supplied by Alexina McWhinnie, had two suggestions to make their propositions workable: that enquirers should be able to see a social worker when applying for this information, especially if they intended to trace their natural parents; that the natural mother should be able to preserve her anonymity, but for the court hearings only, so that her name would be on various records should her child need it in the future.

Although these recommendations were close to the format of the law as it finally emerged six years later, the Houghton Committee was not, at that early stage, completely persuaded by the evidence, as the Working Paper (published late 1970) shows. This argued that adoption should be more open, and accepted the importance of revealing a child's origins, but also stressed the need for anonymity to protect all the parties concerned from future problems.

> Greater openness about adoption does not, however, necessarily entail a knowledge of the actual names of the natural parents and other identifying information. (p.85, para. 234)

> anonymity serves as a protection both for the child and the adoptive parents on the one hand and the natural parents on the other – for the adoptive home against interference from the natural parents or the fear of this; for the natural parents against any temptation to watch the child's progress or in any other way to feel the links still in existence. (p.85, para. 231)[5]

The Working Paper proposed, therefore, that natural parents should be able to remain anonymous if they wished and that access to original birth records in England and Wales should only be granted by permission of a court. The Committee even debated whether or not to withdraw the right of direct access to birth records in Scotland, but decided to defer a decision until the results of Triseliotis's research were available.

The later submission by Triseliotis and others had a considerable effect on the Committee when they systematically reconsidered each of their Working Paper propositions. They accepted that the weight of evidence favoured granting access to birth records in England and Wales and retaining the existing system in Scotland. This almost completely reversed their previous conclusions. They now initially favoured a system which would involve the information being given by a professional social worker, with possibly each application being referred by the Registrar General to a local authority. The Scottish Registrar General was not in favour of this, however, as the involvement of yet another official body might deter future applicants. The Committee avoided getting caught up in a detailed debate at this stage, but the text of their Final Report (1972) made clear the features they thought necessary to make a system of access workable. These were: natural parents should be allowed anonymity until the adoption process was completed; the agency which had arranged the adoption should be obliged to provide a counselling service afterwards to help those adopters who have difficulty in telling their children about their background; the adoption agency be named on the adoption order so that the adoptee would also be able to approach them for further information; adoption agencies retain their records for 75 years; all adoptees in England and Wales be permitted to gain a copy of their original birth entry at the age of 18; the age in Scotland when this law applies be raised to 18; anyone applying for this information be advised that further help would be available from either the adoption agency concerned or the social services; the courts should have the discretion to grant or refuse access to information from the court records of the adoption proceedings.[6]

The Children Act 1975

The Act started life as a Private Member's Bill in 1973, but following the 1974 election the member concerned, Dr David Owen, was appointed Under-Secretary of State for the Social Services in the Department of Health and Social Security. This ensured the successful passage of a new Bill which became the Children Act 1975. A detailed account of the whole process of legislation from 1973 to 1975 is given in the final report of our research.[7] In this section we consider two of the main questions raised in the debates: 'help' to adopted people in search of birth information; and the increasing definition of the legislation regarding access to such information as 'retrospective'. The gradual clarification of the former and the growing realisation of its role in the solution of problems arising from the latter were the two essential elements in the making of Section 26.

The assertion of an adoptee's right of access to birth records was strongly made by Philip Whitehead in the 1973 parliamentary debate on the Houghton Report. A rigorous definition of access to *all* available records, including those of court proceedings, was coupled with a proposal that adopted people should have counselling when they received such information, since at this potentially difficult time the adoptive relationship could be reviewed. The counselling was as much the adopted person's right as access to birth information. Debates on the Children Bill showed that any help to adoptees in relation to access to birth records could be seen in different ways. First, the service could be provided as a way of diverting people or at best making them pause in their search. So, in the second Commons Reading Leo Abse argued that some 'rules' should exist to 'mitigate the consequences' of the applicant having this information, 'by directing these people to some social agency which would erect some barrier, some sifting, before the child went on with his quest. If that is done his need may be assuaged and the possibility of ultimate embarrassment is minimised.'[8] Second, the 'help' envisaged could be seen as a useful reinforcement of reality for the adoptee. In the Standing Committee discussion, for example, Norman Fowler agreed on the necessity for counselling on the grounds that it would enable the adoptee to realise that renewed contact with a natural parent would involve a relationship between two adults; it would not be a reunion of a mother and her young child.[9] No one in the various debates attempted any stock-taking of the different ideas that had emerged, but it is clear that help offered to an adopted person in relation to birth records could have a number of different objectives and be directed towards a number of distinct interests. These differences came to be enshrined in the provision and implementation of Section 26.

Any detailed elaboration of the content of what was being labelled 'counselling' was rendered unnecessary in view of the emerging role of *compulsory* counselling as a solution to the problem of retrospection. This difficulty was raised early in the debates: how could access to birth records apply to those adopted before the Act when natural mothers would until then have placed their child for adoption on the assumption that their child would not be able to trace them? This problem was appreciated by those inside the House and by outside organisations such as the British Association of Social Workers. The difficulty persisted despite arguments that any promise of complete anonymity to natural parents was in fact misconceived, given the then legal position, and that if the relevant clause was not retrospective two groups of adoptees would be created, those with a right of access and those without. The threat of an amendment to make the clause applicable only to those adopted after 1 August 1975 was countered through a change which made counselling *compulsory* for those adopted before 1975 who sought to exercise their right of access to certain birth information. This was not whole-heartedly endorsed by either side of the debate. Mrs Jill Knight, for example, described it 'as a cushion, not a remedy for the worries we have';[9] whilst Dr Owen questioned 'the limitations of this counselling procedure. I think we shall be creating quite an apparatus for a small number of cases.' However, the idea of compulsory counselling was accepted, and Section 26 of the Act made it a duty of the Registrar General, each local authority and each adoption society approved under the Act to provide counselling.

Establishing the counselling service

Establishing a new service on the basis of the Act proved a complex operation. This is not surprising when we consider the background of the provision. This section will discuss only two aspects – the creation of the operational literature of forms and leaflets, and the establishment of the service in the local authorities. The objective in each case is not to provide a detailed chronology but rather to highlight matters of general significance in the making of policy at central and local level.

The operational literature

The forms and leaflets for adoptees and counsellors emerged as a result of joint work throughout 1976 between the Association of British Adoption Agencies (ABAA) the General Registrar Office (GRO) and the Department of Health and Society Security (DHSS). It is inappropriate to consider in any fine detail the various discussions on the happiest wording of sentences, but some of the discussions indicate the presuppositions social actors held as to the nature of the counselling. For example, one of the first questions to be raised by the Association of British Adoption and Fostering Agencies (ABAFA previously ABAA) was whether, to avoid a further application to the courts by the adopted person, the counsellor could supply the name of the placing agency. The DHSS considered that this would not be possible, but the grounds are of interest. The only way the counsellor could obtain the information would be to make that application in advance.

> Two points arise from this. The first is that, in devising the counselling scheme, we have tried to avoid involving the GRO, local authorities or courts in obtaining or giving information which may not be needed. One of the main purposes of the initial (and, it is to be hoped in most cases, the only) interview will be for the counsellor to assess the extent of the applicant's interest in his background. If, as some of the Scottish experience would seem to suggest, he only wishes to satisfy his curiosity about his natural parents, he may be content merely to be given the information that will lead him to his birth record. If, but only if, it becomes evident that the applicant wants more than this, we envisage that the counsellor will either offer to get the name of the agency or local authority or suggest that the applicant apply to the court himself.[10]

The role of the GRO and local authority is envisaged as fairly limited, probably involving only one interview and referring the applicant on to other sources of information if required. It was not thought that the counsellors themselves would be involved either in searching out or in disclosing more detailed information. The 'if, but only if' is a vivid expression of the exiguous nature of the DHSS' view.

This picture of the counsellor's task underwent alteration during the drafting of the 'Notes for Counsellors'. In general, the drafting of the leaflets both for counsellors and applicants proved to be more difficult than at first thought because of the complicated legal processes and documentation involved in birth registration and adoption. It was also considered that the content of both leaflets should correspond since some adoptees might obtain copies of the leaflet for counsellors. The counsellors' leaflet described the purpose of counselling as:

> to ensure (1) that the adopted person has considered the possible effect of any enquiries both on himself and on others: and (2) that the information he seeks, and to which he now has a legal right, is provided in a helpful and appropriate manner.[11]

As well as describing the application procedure, the Notes also described the 'Tools for Counselling', which were a familiarity with adoption practice and procedures and a knowledge of the difference between the various birth certificates. The 'role of the counsellor' was said to be 'important but limited', though how limited would depend on the applicant's wishes. Such an attitude to the 'counsellee' as determining the limits of 'help' is interesting in view of the total disregard of anything the counselling literature might say.

The preparation of forms and leaflets raised other issues besides the role of the counsellor and the content of counselling. For example, what was the position of British adoptees living abroad? Ideas of postal counselling had been earlier dismissed, so how would such people acquire their original birth certificates? One possible solution was for the local authority or agency, from whom that person would be entitled to receive counselling, to delegate the counselling to another organisation, namely the International Social Services. This would apparently have involved a great deal of liaison, and the DHSS expressed unhappiness about the apparent shifting of the 'martyr's' role:

> we have led local authorities to believe that one of the purposes in setting up the GRO's counselling unit was to enable the central body to bear the brunt of the new counselling system.

As it turned out, however, the local authorities did not have any jurisdiction outside their own areas and were, therefore, unable legally to delegate counselling in this way. Consequently, adoptees living abroad had to return to Great Britain to receive counselling under the same system as other applicants.

We have seen that Section 26 was conceived as some kind of protective service. Discussion at one stage in the preparation of documents turned to the possibility of counsellors tracing natural parents to forewarn them if they thought they would be contacted by the adopted person. It was suggested that an easy way of tracing would be to use the National Health Service Central Records, which record changes both in names and addresses of anyone registered with a doctor. Some alarm was expressed at this. All medical records were confidential, but also publicising a system which could be used to trace individuals very easily was the subject of considerable apprehension.

These two issues – the position of British adoptees living abroad, and the possibility of forewarning natural parents – serve to emphasise different aspects of the legislation. The first shows the importance attached to the one face-to-face interview, so that people living abroad have to travel to Britain if they want their birth certificate information. The second illustrates how easy it is to trace someone using official sources (National Insurance numbers are another example) but how difficult it is for an adopted person who has to rely on old, maybe incomplete, records. This is not to suggest that the authorities should trace natural parents on the adoptee's behalf, but to point out that the issue was clearly one of conflicting rights. This was resolved by giving adoptees partial rather than total access to information. The information also referred to the past and parents in the past, rather than to their present circumstances. We can envisage this, rather than the counselling, as more reassuring to those people who objected to the retrospective nature of the legislation. There is also an element of testing the applicant's motivation in both sets of circumstances, since most would have to be serious about their intentions to discover information and/or trace parents if it involved either a journey from abroad or a long, arduous search on their own.

The establishment of the local authority service
Section 26 was implemented on 26 November 1976. Little systematic information is available on the extent and nature of

discussions within authorities but results of our survey, conducted in January 1981, provide some evidence of the experience of local authorities in the early days of Section 26 and the range of organisational arrangements. All authorities were circulated and a very high response rate of 94.8 per cent was obtained.

Respondents were asked to provide information about the early days of Section 26, the nature of discussions about implementation, the importance accorded to Section 26, and whether extra resources were allocated. Authorities were also asked to describe their current (1981) arrangements for Section 26, which in most cases were the same arrangements settled upon after discussions at the time of implementation. (Of the 53 authorities which reported changes in organisation since 1976, the majority concerned routine change of personnel.) Full details of the methodology and findings are given in Haimes and Timms (1983). We present here the material relevant to a general discussion of implementation, namely, how decisions about implementation and organisation illuminate the image of counselling and access to birth records held by those responsible for such decisions.

It would appear that Section 26 was not regarded initially as a vitally important piece of work by most local authorities. Only 34 regarded it as 'very important'. Decisions about implementation were made at directorate level in 74 authorities, but this was more a sign of formality than of importance. This relatively low-key re-action contrasts with that of the legislators and the public in general who devoted more attention to the law on access than most other sections in the Act. Perhaps those who were more involved in the day-to-day maintenance of child care in social services departments saw access as less important than other sections of the Act. However, it would be wrong to suggest that authorities dismissed Section 26 as unimportant, rather it was not singled out for special attention from the rest of the Act. Most authorities appear not to have thought extra resources were necessary for implementing Section 26. Fifty-one regarded extra resources as unnecessary and only 12 authorities allocated extra resources, varying from financing attendance at training courses to payment for counselling on a sessional basis. No one knew – neither the local authorities, the DHSS nor the GRO – quite how many applications were to be expected, so 17 authorities deferred making a decision about extra resources until the level of demand could be calculated. Although the study in Scotland indicated that demand would be low there was a general fear that the amount of publicity given to the Act would stimulate a flood of applications. Even so, most authorities considered their present level of manpower was adequate, and there were no echoes of any earlier anxieties about the level of skill required.

In terms of the organisation of counselling most authorities followed the advice of a DHSS circular, or deemed it appropriate by their own judgement to allocate the role to specific individuals, who would be known throughout the authority as holding that responsibility. At least 98 out of the 110 local authorities responding to the questionnaire delegated counselling to particular individuals, and only nine appeared to treat Section 26 applicants for allocation on a normal case-load basis. The tone of the circular and of debates prior to implementation had some influence, in as much as the largest single group of the delegating authorites (44 authorities) allocated the task to adoption specialists. Another 11 authorities gave adoptions officers a supervisory role in relation either to child care specialists or to generic social workers. Not every authority had adoption specialists to call on, of course, since most local authorities did not function as adoption agencies. In this case counselling was allocated to child care specialists, generic social workers and various other combinations. It seems that only one authority took the advice of the circular to delegate counselling to an outside organisation, a voluntary adoption agency which performed all their adoption work and so assumed the counselling role as well. One other authority employed an outside help with the counselling; a university lecturer, ex-child care worker, who had more experience than most of the personnel in the adoption unit of that authority.

Several authorities were undergoing a period of transition when Section 26 was implemented and adoption was particularly open to development as authorities foresaw the eventual implementation of Section 1 of the 1975 Act, which required a comprehensive adoption service. (At least 16 authorities have become adoption agencies since 1975.) The period of upheaval was used by some of the more senior social workers in managerial roles to establish both Section 26 as work requiring a high standard of practice and certain standards of practice in their adoption work as a whole. Several senior officers mentioned in later interviews that Section 26 constituted important opportunities to form links between headquarters staff and area workers, to identify existing skills and to develop interest in an area of work which would later require experienced staff.

Turning now to where the counsellors were based, out of the 98 delegating authorities, 33 delegated as counsellors social workers who were based in area teams, and another 20 had counsellors based both in area and central offices; 44 authorities had counsellors based in central offices only. This illustrates the connection between any specialist work and a central base which is a feature of other aspects of social work in a local authority. The largest single group of workers assigned the counselling task were adoption specialists and the majority of these were based centrally as single individuals, or as groups forming adoption units. The majority of counsellors based in area teams were generic social workers, and the majority of the authorities which had counsellors based both in area and central offices operated a system whereby counsellors were not adoption specialists but were supervised by an adoptions officer. Some authorities had no history of centrally-based specialists, so the work was immediately allocated to area social workers. In other authorities area-based counsellors were considered necessary given the size and rural nature of the authority, such that travelling to a central office would be difficult for applicants. However, in one authority which had little tradition of centrally-based specialists the very fact that Section 26 was used to establish a central adoption unit was seen as a mark of its imporance. Other authorities were less concerned with existing structures and were more interested in appointing social workers who had what were deemed to be the appropriate skills, described by a member of one authority as experience in family work and past practice such that the situation of all parties at the time of adoption could be described to the applicant. A representative of another authority said he appointed counsellors on the basis of their philosophy on adoption, their knowledge of adoption and their experience in 'child care counselling': these people might be based either in areas or in central offices.

In authorities where counsellors were area-based generic workers delicate negotiations had sometimes to be conducted between central and area managerial staff to ensure that adequate priority was given to Section 26 work. Some authorities reported a resentment amongst social workers who opposed Section 26 on the grounds that it put the profession in a position of 'breaking faith' with natural parents because of its retrospective nature. There was some initial reluctance to allocate sufficient manpower resources for the adequate performance of the task. Even though this does not appear to have been a major problem, the question of resources remained, particularly in area teams, because of the nature of the work. Since it rarely entailed emergency action or involved crises at any time, and since it was seen as very enjoyable work, it was in some areas seen as low-priority work. Area-based counsellors were not always given reduction in their case loads to compensate for their Section 26 commitments.

The main organisational features of the implementation of Section 26 can be summarised in the following groupings of authorities:

Group 1:   those delegating Section 26 work to only one counsellor (16);

Group 2:   those delegating Section 26 work to adoption specialists, but with more than one counsellor (35);

Group 3:   those delegating Section 26 work to a combination of adoptions officers and other types of social workers (21);

Group 4:   those delegating Section 26 work to non-adoption specialists (26);

Group 5:   those not delegating Section 26 work to named individuals (9);

Group 6:   those with a mixed system of delegating some but not all Section 26 work to named individuals (3).

The authorities in Group 5 tended to allocate cases according to the area in which the applicant lived. These cases were then distributed on the normal case-load basis and dealt with by a variety of social workers within the authority. The three authorities in Group 6 appear to have a mixed system because of the autonomy of the area offices within the authority as a whole. Thus, some areas chose to designate a particular social worker as Section 26 counsellor and others did not. Members of both these groupings appear not to conform with the desired features of Section 26 counselling as described in the various circulars, that is, they are apparently not allowing for the build-up of counselling experience within a particular group of individuals which, it was thought, would lead to an improved service. The same could be said for those authorities in Group 1, which operate with the extreme opposite system, that is, only one person in the whole authority does the counselling. Whilst that person is clearly becoming very experienced in the work, the benefit of that experience is not shared by others, so the authority is dependent on that person remaining in post to retain an experienced counsellor. Several counsellors expressed concern at this weakness in the system.

One of the main concerns expressed by the ABAA in terms of local authority counselling was whether there would be sufficient depth of experience and counselling skills available in all authorities. In as much as most authorities could appoint designated counsellors this could be said to be evidence that such skills existed. However, as we have already seen, authorities differed in what they deemed to be appropriate or at least sufficient skills for Section 26 work. The majority did tend to see it located within adoption work, and this was more important in decisions over designation than concerns with skills in counselling. Local authorities, therefore, felt they had enough personnel able to perform the task adequately or at least the personnel to ensure that the task was performed adequately by others. This might explain why the most common form of training made available to Section 26 counsellors took the form of in-service discussions. Counsellors in effect trained themselves using the booklets and their own previous experiences to alert themselves to the dangers and difficulties that could arise. Only 14 authorities reported attendance at outside training courses. Generally speaking, the innovation of Section 26 was incorporated within existing child care and adoption experience and expertise.

Although in most authorities the number of applications did not reach the expected target, several mentioned that the amount of work involved in individual cases had exceeded their expectations. This point will be expanded later, but for some counsellors, especially those who are the only counsellor in an authority, the work has been much heavier than expected. If their superiors expected that counselling would be a simple one-off interview, as many did after reading the circulars and the various debates, conflict might arise, and has arisen, over the amount of the individual's time devoted to counselling. The most serious problems to arise, however, have been the lack of information available for some applicants and the non-cooperation of courts in releasing information. Many counsellors expected, as did the DHSS (evidenced by the circular sent to local authorities), that the guardian *ad litem* reports would be made available for applicants who wanted more than just the birth certificate information. Authorities who hold copies of these reports do, in fact, often release that information to applicants, but the courts who are sometimes the only holders of the forms do not release them. This was first raised in the very early days of implementation in 1977 and the legal ruling given was that the reports were the possession of the courts, not the individual or authority responsible for compiling them. Disclosure of information from them could in fact constitute contempt of court. The courts were allowed to disclose under changed rules only the name of the placing agency. Even though this matter was apparently settled by the judgment in 1977, the problem still recurs and appears to be a source of serious present frustration to most counsellors.

The difficulty over the release of information from the guardian *ad litem* report epitomises the ambiguity inherent in the law: is the law on access and the provision of counselling a law for the provision of information, or a law for the protection of natural parents? We have seen in this chapter various definitions of the purpose of counselling, from the ABAA's suggestion in January 1975 that counselling should be provided for the benefit of the adopted person to explore feelings about adoption, to later definitions (from the GRO and in the DHSS circular) that counselling should either put adoptees off tracing natural parents or at the very least warn them of the dangers of so doing. Concurrent with these sentiments was the assumption, or even perhaps hope, that if information was provided adoptees would be less likely to want to trace (based on findings of the Scottish study). However, the letter of the law allowed only limited information to be released, that which would lead to the birth certificate. Whilst providing for access to other sources of information, through the provision of counselling from adoption agencies and the release of the name of that agency if not previously known, the release of the extra information was not made mandatory.

References

(1)   Adoption Act 1950, p.523.

(2)   Hurst Report, 1954, p.53.

(3)   Appendix to Home Office Letter, HO 58/59, March 1959.

(4)   Houghton Committee Minutes (Meeting of 24 November 1969).

(5)   Houghton Committee Working Paper (HMSO, 1970, p.85, paras 234 and 231).

(6)   Houghton Committee Report (HMSO, 1972).

(7)   Haimes, E. and Timms, N. (1983) *Final Report to the DHSS*.

(8)   Hansard, v.893, c.1821–1924.

(9)   Hansard, Parliamentary Debates, Commons, Standing Committee A, Session 1974–5, vol. 1.

(10)   Correspondence between DHSS and ABAFA, 1 March 1976.

(11)   HMSO (1976) 'Access to birth records: notes for counsellors'.

(12)   DHSS (1976) Local authority circular (76) 21.

3 Social Workers as Counsellors

The Barclay Report (1982) stated that 'counselling was one of the main elements in social work', but it did not argue the case in detail, and its hold on the concept was not strengthened by any empirical inquiry. The Committee had not apparently noticed that through Section 26 of the 1975 Children Act counselling was made a part of social work in relation to certain adoptees. This counselling was accepted without argument as appropriate work for social workers, and they brought to it a great deal of experience in 'traditional' child care social work. Our study of social workers as Section 26 counsellors shows the practitioners in relation to the organisation and administration of a particular service, but it also illuminates the context in which counselling is made for delivery as a service. Counselling devoid of such a context may constitute a service offered by the private practitioner: it forms no part of social work.

The majority of social workers involved in Section 26 counselling are people with a considerable degree of experience in 'child care' social work. Most local authorities, as we have seen, delegate the work to particular personnel who have this experience. Even where work is distributed to the area teams for the usual allocation it is invariably picked up by social workers expressing an interest in adoption. This wealth of experience was used in the construction of the new service Section 26 constituted for adopted people. The social workers we interviewed claimed that experience of what they termed 'the whole spectrum of adoption' from dealing with natural mothers to placing children with approved adopters was a necessary requirement for effective counselling. Experience of this work enabled social workers to undertake with greater confidence the task of recreating for adopted people the historical circumstances in which their natural parents' decision to place them for adoption might be more understandable. (The spectrum described by counsellors, incorporating the three parties 'traditionally' recognised could, of course, be extended to involve the whole social nature and significance of adoption.) It was also felt by social workers who expressed most concern about the 'broken promise' aspect of the retrospective legislation that it was appropriate that those who had played some part in earlier work with natural parents should be involved. In a sense, work under Section 26, they believed, was *owed* to natural parents.

However, counselling adopted people concerning their birth records was significantly connected by the social workers to the context of the total adoption service in ways other than the historical. The work of Section 26 was seen as presently influencing the shape of contemporary practice in adoption. Just over half the local authorities replied that the work fitted well with and informed the rest of adoption service. The social workers had evidently reflected on the results of bad practice in the past and also on the importance for adopted people of the kind and range of information that might be gathered and preserved at the time of the adoption. One social worker instanced how she had initiated as a new policy in the department more determined attempts to trace and interview natural fathers because of the future significance any information thus gained held for the adopted person.

So far the belief of practitioners in the place of Section 26 in the spectrum of adoption service has been illustrated, but Section 26 should also be seen within the context of social work. It illustrates how a new aspect of social work has evolved. The law itself and guidance from central government obviously provided groundwork for the new service, but the detail of the construction required devising. In examining the structure of the operant service it seems that a number of factors were significant. First, the task was deemed a suitable one for social workers. This is not to say that all social workers necessarily agreed with the law nor that social workers expressed no resentment at being given by parliament a task of great complexity and some ambiguity. Whatever the problems, Section 26 was unambiguously accepted as part of social work, and so it appeared to Members of Parliament and to organisations like the Association of Directors of Social Service.

It is, of course, possible to envisage the use of other kinds of personnel, such as specially recruited lay people or those with legal training, and we discussed this in our interviews with the social workers. One admitted that a lawyer could conduct a Section 26 interview, but added:

it would be quite a detached interview and clinical. Purely imparting information without really thinking about the kind of impact it may have on the recipient. . . . I think perhaps social workers are more sensitive to people's feelings and can perhaps pick up anxieties and concerns more than say a lawyer . . . who wouldn't have time to do it apart from anything else.

The other factors that were important in the construction of the new service were the past and current experience of practitioners operating the provision at the 'client' face, the administrative framework of local authority service, and the procedures and guidelines to be found in the booklets issued by the DHSS. Professional experience and administrative advice and regulation together constituted the base from which the counselling was made.

At this point, it is worth considering those factors that did *not* play a role in the construction of the new service. Despite a local authority circular (LAC(76)21) which drew a parallel between Section 26 counselling and 'counselling' in other areas of social work, no attempt was made to build the service around a consideration of possible similarities and differences between the kinds of counselling undertaken by social workers. Particular theories of counselling were not advanced nor did anyone raise as a question sufficiency in numbers of *counsellors*, even though the 1975 Act was the first to use the terms 'counselling' and 'counsellor'. The practitioners in our selection hesitated over these terms, recognised some of the implicit problems, but considered that they could and perhaps should be held somehow in abeyance whilst the 'real' work continued. 'Counselling' and 'counsellor' were as problematic as 'social work' and 'social worker', but such problems were worthy of simple acknowledgement rather than pragmatic attention.

I know there's a lot said about social work – this approach and that approach, you know, but I think you do what they [the adopted people] need you to do at that time. Just because adoption counselling is a title, it isn't a set of rules. . . . It's using whatever's needed for that person.

So, a consideration of the construction of Section 26 counselling may help to illuminate the apparently vexed question concerning the identity of social work. The counselling service was constructed on an administrative and legal basis and on the experience of social workers who respond to what they see as need in an appropriate manner. What social workers actually do, and indeed what they have done since the beginning of modern social work, is not, at one level, deeply problematic: they deliver and help to deliver various services, they listen, they make suggestions and arrangements. What

is problematic and complex are the judgements of appropriateness
and the apparent denial of the place of any rules. Social workers
often find it difficult to elaborate the simple description of listening,
contacting other agencies, and so on, because they are seldom
helped to discern those features of a situation that justify one activity
as more appropriate than another. Examining the structure of
Section 26 counselling that has come to be devised by social work
practitioners presents in miniature a process that has central
significance for an understanding of the making of social work.

The service: progressing through stages

Whatever the intention of legislators and administrators with regard
to Section 26 – as a barrier, brake or simply a place and space for
moral and psychological hesitation – social workers act on an
assumption that each applicant has the potential of following a
linear progression from simply obtaining the birth certificate information to meeting and making contact with a natural parent. It is
not assumed that every applicant will pursue this path as far as a
meeting with a natural parent nor that every applicant ought to do
so. Each applicant, however, is considered in the light of the
complete progression in which the following steps are identified:

  (i)   to apply under Section 26 for information of the original
         birth certificate;
 (ii)   to send off for a copy of that birth certificate;
(iii)   to apply to the court for the name of the placing agency;
 (iv)   to apply to that agency for further information regarding
         that placement;
  (v)   to attempt to trace the natural parent(s) and/or siblings;
 (vi)   to make contact with the natural parent(s);
(vii)   to meet the natural parent(s);
(viii)   to maintain contact.

The tasks of the counsellor are seen in relation to each of these
stages:

then I go on to explaining really what my role as a counsellor is,
vis-à-vis their application to the GRO, and follow some of that
through, that . . . we can provide basic information or we can try
and delve further, and also explaining that really my role is to act
as a counsellor for that person, but also perhaps potentially, in the
end to act as an intermediary.

Consequently, it is appropriate to describe the counselling service as seen by the practitioners in a similarly linear progression: the stages into which the counselling service can be analysed and the decisions inherent in them.

The 'complete' sequence, which starts, of course, before an applicant is seen, can be envisaged as follows: administration on receiving a new case; arranging an appointment with the applicant and deciding the location; holding the statutory counselling interview and imparting the birth certificate information and the form for application to the court for the name of the placing agency; maintaining contact with the applicants; tracing further information and natural parent(s); contacting natural parent(s); arranging a meeting between applicant and natural parent(s); maintaining contact between applicant and/or natural parent(s) if appropriate. Few counsellors will perform all the tasks in relation to the same applicant, but awareness of the potential sequence affects the conduct of the stages that are performed. A detailed discussion of each stage can be found in Haimes and Timms (1983). In this work we outline some of the main features.

Administration of a new 'case'

What appears significant in the way the early handling of the application is organised is the distinctiveness of the service. The first a local authority hears about a case is when an envelope arrives, usually addressed to the Director whose name has been given to the applicant, containing a set of papers relating to complete strangers. In authorities with an adoption unit the papers are handled separately from all other new cases coming to the department; they are filed separately, either with the adoption files or even separately from these. Even in authorities with no established adoption work great emphasis is placed on confidentiality and the records of completed Section 26 work are usually returned to the centre rather than being stored in the area office.

The difference between the handling of Section 26 cases and other new work is again evident when we consider the question of checking existing departmental records to discover if the applicant has been a client of the department or if any files connected with the adoption are available. About half the counsellors interviewed checked on the latter, though practice varied on how much use was made of any information in the first interview, since there is no legal requirement to pass on information gained from that source. One counsellor, describing a routine check to see if the applicant was 'known' as a current client of the department, explained, 'if they were a mental health client, for instance, that might have repercussions on their motivation for finding out their antecedents.' This counsellor described this check as 'an automatic safety net', but it is not used by the majority of counsellors. As another counsellor said, 'I made a point of keeping an open mind' about the applicant, and he felt that as a consequence his interviews were more open and honest as the applicant was not left wondering what else the social worker knew. Others argued that 'they have the right to keep that bit of their life completely separate', and that if information of that kind was discovered accidentally, 'I would put that aside, that has nothing to do with it.' In these instances any previous identity as 'client' is judged to be irrelevant. This would not be the practice in relation to other users of local authority social services.

Arranging the interview
We have already seen that Section 26 work is attended by rather special considerations of confidentiality, and that differences are made from the beginning between this and other work. These features are also apparent when we consider the making of arrangements for the interview. Applicants are informed that they should contact the local authority, and some counsellors believe that it is appropriate to await such contact, particularly since nothing is known of the applicant's home circumstances and an initiative on the part of the social worker might appear to broach confidential material. It is usual, of course, in other situations for counsellors to await an approach, but this parallel significantly was not drawn by many of our respondents. Some social workers indeed argued that many applicants have had to 'screw up their courage' to take the initial steps and that a lack of response on the part of the local authority might be detrimental.

Most interviews are arranged to take place in the local authority offices. Some counsellors defined the office as 'neutral territory', whilst others thought that applicants themselves were happier in an office free from interruptions. To the research interviewer as an outsider, however, few of the offices appeared as neutral, private or free from interruption, though such adjectives perhaps come easily to those who know their surroundings well enough to ignore them. Of greater interest perhaps are the professional grounds used to justify the choice of location of the interview. Most counsellors express a routine preference for interviews in the office. The office appointment 'is usually the principle in adoption work – they want something from you, they come and get it.' This in itself is one way in which adoption cases are thought to require out of the ordinary treatment. It seems that it is the 'first' interview which is regarded in the ways we have described, since many second and subsequent interviews are conducted in the applicant's home, as if, once the critical first interview has been completed, different considerations apply. The first interview seems in fact to operate ambiguously: as some kind of test (of motivation, for example) and also as an expression of the principle of self-determination.

Conducting the counselling interview

The typical interview 'as it emerges', closely resembles that outlined in 'Notes for Counsellors', though most counsellors say they do not refer to this booklet after conducting the first two or three interviews. The Notes outline three possible interviews: an applicant who only wants the birth certificate information; one wanting more information but not wishing to trace natural parents; an applicant who wishes to trace natural parents. In the first case the counsellor is urged to be sensitive to the applicant's wishes and warned that not all the GRO information need be given if it is not wanted. In the second, the applicant might need to discuss why he wants to know more and request advice as to where other information might be available. The counsellor should be willing to help the applicant obtain the information, provided the intitative comes from the applicant. For the interview in which an applicant might want to trace natural parents the counsellor has 'a responsibility to discuss the implications of such a search while conveying an understanding of the applicant's needs and feelings.'

Usually, the counsellor begins by asking about the amount of information the adoptees already possess about their background, followed by an enquiry about what more they wish to know, and why. The first question often suffices – the details 'pour out'. Counsellors differ concerning the point in the interview at which they give the birth certificate information. Some give it after their initial questions, but most prefer to go on to discuss the implications of having the information before they give it. What appears as a major determinant is the degree of difficulty in holding the applicant's attention: if the applicant appears impatient or unwilling to talk the information may be given after the first round of questions in the hope that any reaction to the information can be used in further discussion, though such a tactic is not without its risks:

I remember one man who came in who was rather aggressive and didn't want to lead gradually up to it, which I would prefer to do, and more or less said, 'You've got the birth certificate, can I see it?' So I showed it to him . . . then started a bit of patter and he just ignored me – he didn't want to discuss it.

Most applicants seem to have considered fully the implications of the information they are about to receive, and this is a subject for surprise, at least on the part of some counsellors:

We'll go on to talk about some of the problems of tracing natural parents. But I do find most people have already thought about these things. It always amazes me how sensible in fact people are.

(The social worker here was referring to the adopted people she had seen and not to people in general.) Section 26 has produced for social workers people who are almost defined as clients but whose personal characteristics do not resemble those of the social worker's usual clientele. Most applicants have also considered the possible effects of their present and possible future actions and are not viewed by counsellors as 'hell-bent' on tracing their natural parents, but as 'very normal and well-balanced' and, whilst perhaps nervous at seeing a social worker, well able to cope with receiving the information. None the less, counsellors feel in duty bound to discuss all the possible implications, 'to go through my patter' as one described it. The 'Notes for Counsellors' indicate, as we have seen, that in cases where it is likely the adopted person will search for the natural parent(s), 'The counsellor has a responsibility to discuss the implications of such a search, while conveying an understanding of the applicant's needs and feelings.' Sometimes, of course, the apparent distinction between 'discussing implications' and 'understanding need' cannot be easily managed, for instance in cases where applicants express a need to search. Most counsellors adopt a similar response in interpreting the guidance. They advise the adoptee of the possible *outcomes* of the search, usually emphasising negative possibilities. Thus, no records may be available; the natural mother may refuse a meeting; a meeting may be arranged but there is no guarantee that the parties will actually like each other; or a now elderly natural parent may become dependent on the adoptee's family.

The information enabling the applicants to apply for the original birth certificate is usually given at the conclusion of the 'implications' phase of the interview. This information comprises the applicant's original name and the name of the natural mother and of the natural father if this has been recorded. The information is entered on a form in the counsellor's possession so that the applicants, if they wish, can apply for the original certificate. The counsellor may also give the applicant authorisation to request from the court the name of the placing agency. The amount of discussion at this point depends on the applicant's reaction, but counsellors attempt some discussion at least to round off the interview in case it should prove to be a 'once-and-only' and to indicate the possibility of further meetings.

Further contact and tracing

Involvement between counsellors and applicants following the statutory interview is carefully negotiated: the applicant is not compelled to attend and the social workers can be subjected to organisational and professional pressure to limit their work:

> I have been told that I *mustn't* help people with their search by the 'powers that be', you know, that it's too much of an investment of my time, it's time-consuming. But, not for these reasons but for my own reasons, I think that's right . . . what I do is advise them [the applicants].

Decisions about further involvement and the nature of the involvement usually rest on the applicants' intentions. If they appear entirely happy with the information and express no present desire to go further, the counsellor will invite the applicant to renew contact in the future if they wish, but otherwise leaves the matter there. Counsellors rarely regard it as their function to 'chase up' applicants, though they might well actively pursue other 'clients'. Experience of the research led some to question how far applicants believed in the counsellor's 'Come back if you want any further help'. In the words of one counsellor,

> because you're doing this research I've been in touch with two people who I haven't contacted and they haven't contacted me. And both are wanting more contact. And that's quite interesting actually, that they didn't feel that they could come back.

In many situations, however, applicants are clear about wanting to gain more information and possibly to trace natural parents, and they welcome the support and advice of the counsellor. In these cases there is often a division of labour between counsellor and applicant, but counsellors disagree on the amount of help that should be given at this stage. Those who take on a fairly large share justify themselves on professional and practical grounds. The 'extra' work is seen as a logical extension of their responsibilities as counsellors; by remaining closely involved they are more likely to be used as an intermediary in any meeting with natural parents. Moreover, it is in the nature of the case easier for the counsellor to gain access to the records of other organisations. Most counsellors, however, believe that it is not their function to trace natural parents for the applicants: they must display appropriate motivation and take on the task themselves: 'I was only there to enable it to happen if that's what they wanted. I tried not to become too involved . . . that's just being plain nosey.'

Acting as intermediary

The majority of counsellors interviewed have acted as intermediaries for the applicants making contact with a natural parent, invariably the mother. Others have asked social workers in other areas to make contact for them. The task of acting as intermediary is not particularly easy for social workers: one very experienced counsellor described it as 'much more unnerving than anything else I've had to do.'

Two kinds of problem emerge: the tactical and the ethical. How should the contact be made – by telephone, letter or a personal visit? Most counsellors prefer to send a letter, allowing the receiver time to recover from the shock in private and protecting themselves from an unwelcome reaction. A visit to the natural parent, either shortly after, or instead of, a letter presents fewer problems to counsellors less anxious over confidentiality, but other problems can arise. One counsellor called on a natural mother and introduced herself as from the social services. Wishing to broach the topic with care, she asked if a particular date had any significance. Unfortunately it did not, and after a lengthy explanation that she was not calling about her pension or the home help or the meals-on-wheels, she had to come 'straight out with it'.

Partly because of these practical difficulties, and partly for ethical reasons, counsellors express mixed feelings about the intermediary function. The ethical considerations weigh most heavily with those counsellors who in the past had themselves told natural mothers that the child would never be able to trace them. In a sense they indirectly encouraged natural parents to keep the adoption a secret but are now in the position of telling these parents that they can no longer hide the truth. Making contact produces anxiety in all parties concerned and they start 'making all sorts of judgements about themselves in their real situations'. These counsellors argue that natural parents should have some rights of protection and should have the right to refuse to meet the applicant without undue pressure. When a refusal occurs, counsellors will often spend more time with both applicant and parents, helping them to recover from the shock or disappointment and getting them to see each other's point of view. The work with parents is also described as counselling.

The positive side to acting as an intermediary is seen in the number of happy reunions that occur. Counsellors can see their role as contributing to a successful outcome which might have been otherwise if the applicants had searched and made contact by themselves. They sometimes wonder if perhaps they are too protective of natural parents and that the risks to them from disturbed applicants are actually very small. Whilst the counsellor should try to protect people from unnecessary intrusions into their lives, the existence of counselling and the possibility of an intermediary may be judged sufficient protection for natural parents. As one counsellor said, 'The right of people to know who they are overrides the right of natural parents to complete privacy.'

Conclusion

The provision of Section 26 appears on the statute book as comparatively simple and discrete. In this chapter we have tried to describe the detail and the complexity of the service that has emerged. The counselling work has been described in terms of a sense of connected steps. At each step we can see the service in its operational detail and as the result of the working of a number of factors, including the administrative framework provided by local and central government and the professional discretion of experienced social workers as they judge on the appropriate action. We turn in the next chapter to consider the major problems described by counsellors and the solutions commonly adopted. These, too, have helped in the formation of the counselling service.

4 Problems and Solutions in Birth Record Counselling

The problems posed by Section 26 counselling and the solutions reached by social workers have implications both for the social organisation of adoption and also for counselling as a generic part of social work. It may appear initially that counselling, social work and the operation of Section 26 present few problems – social workers respond to adopted people as they express their needs. Yet, as we have seen, the history and the immediate intentions of those framing and supporting Section 26 lead to ambiguous and ambivalent interpretations of the provision. Moreover, the term 'counselling' cannot be ignored, and as practitioners attempt to align concept and activity certain problems emerge. This chapter is concerned with problems in the conception and the boundaries of the counselling service. Problems of the identity of the service and of its 'clients', and questions of 'how far should a counsellor go' appear to be solved by the social workers concerned in two main ways: explicitly through the use of professional judgement in the exercise of discretion, and implicitly through the employment of distinct strategies.

The problems which are central to the operation of the service can be highlighted in summary form through contrasting some general notions of counselling with the activities required under Section 26. Counsellors do not seem to use any particular theory of counselling, but the problems they describe can be interpreted as arising from some kind of clash between Section 26 work and an implicit general model of the activities called 'counselling'. Thus, counselling is often seen as a listening activity untrammelled by other functions, but in Section 26 it is set alongside the giving of certain information to which the applicant has a right. Questions concerning the balance between these activities may arise. Counselling is usually undertaken in relation to a problem which a client voluntarily brings to the counsellor, whereas under Section 26 there is compulsion, the problem is ambiguous, and the status of 'client' is weakly established. Counselling is an activity finely tuned to the individual and proceeds at a pace appropriate to him, but under Section 26 attempts may be made to regulate the pace by the need to safeguard the interests of others. The problems expressed in these contrasts will be discussed under two headings: Counselling and the giving of information, and How far should the counsellor go?

Counselling and the giving of information

Interestingly enough, counsellors invariably talked of applicants in terms of 'why they have come for counselling' rather than why they had come for the information. This was not because giving the information was seen as some kind of administrative chore, far from it, since social workers usually prepared themselves with care in relation to the information-giving aspects of their interviews. It is rather that 'counselling' seems to operate as a powerful force pulling counsellors towards 'problems'. This happens at three levels. First, the use of the term suggests a difficulty or problem that is at least temporarily beyond solution, but, as several Section 26 counsellors pointed out, the applicants we were studying had had their problem and at least part of its solution (obtaining birth information) defined for them 'as being adopted and wanting information'. Thus 'counselling' seems at least to suggest a close association between 'being adopted' and 'having problems', even though Section 26 gives applicants the right to certain birth information and, as we shall see, social workers believe that such a right should be upheld.

Second, problems could become apparent in the way that certain applicants made use of Section 26. Those who did not disclose their feelings were described as 'superficial' or even 'cocky, self-sufficient', and concern was expressed about those who seemed to be coping with everything in a manner described as 'too good'. One applicant who had followed the parliamentary debates on access to birth records was described by the counsellor as someone who 'functions with the brains best', and as having all the answers to questions 'absolutely right'. The social worker would have felt easier with someone more prepared to disclose his feelings. Most applicants expressed their feelings with relative ease, and this enabled counsellors to discern problems at a third level through judgements about their coping capacities and motivation. Sometimes those judged not to be coping well could be helped within the somewhat ill-defined boundaries of counselling, but for others this presented much more difficulty.

One fairly definitive group of applicants identified as not coping well were older applicants who reported unhappy adoptions, a lack of discussion about adoption and a feeling of a lack of identity. Feelings of disloyalty and guilt towards adoptive parents were also seen as a particular problem for this group. Counsellors feared that they might feel much more for their natural parents if they were to meet them. On the other hand, counsellors suspected that many of these applicants had never recovered from a sense of rejection by their natural mother and that they were trying to come to terms with this by finding out the circumstances surrounding their adoption. Although concerned for and by such applicants, counsellors felt they could do something positive for them. They could either sit back and listen to the feelings expressed, and so help the person to sort out exactly what they felt about whom; alternatively, they could help them to trace records or explain some of the history of adoption practice, so that the position of both natural and adoptive parents at the time of placement was better understood.

Another, smaller group of applicants created anxiety largely because counsellors felt that there was little they could do for them. This group has a wide range of characteristics – such as being very young, or angry or unstable – but the common features were a certain failure in discussion and a determination to seek out their natural parents. 'Non-talking' was not always seen by counsellors as a problem if they considered that the applicant had an alternative source of support. Failure to discuss, however, must in terms of Section 26 and of any conception of counselling present the social worker with a serious problem. This is succinctly conveyed in the following description of one applicant:

> She was absolutely like a rock you couldn't penetrate. There was no way she could have gone out of here saying she'd been counselled. I mean, I said all the right things . . . but she was absolutely determined to go . . . and seek out her real mother.

Given Section 26 the counsellor could not, nor did he wish to, withhold birth certificate information; on the other hand, such counselling seems almost the equivalent of following the rules about what should be said.

In this section we have seen the problems which may arise at different levels through the use of counselling as a medium for the delivery of certain information. These problems, as we shall see, are solved more or less satisfactorily. However, for one particular group of potential users of Section 26 it does appear that the means (counselling) has become primary in relation to the ends (access to birth information). We refer to people adopted in England and Wales but now living abroad. The present position is that in such cases access to birth information will only be granted if the applicant is able to attend for a counselling session in this country.

How far should the counsellor go?

Counselling can be seen as 'the medium of the message'; it can also be seen as pursuing two distinct aims: meeting the needs of adopted people through making enquiries about their origins, and also providing a safeguard. This twofold activity is not uncommon in other aspects of social work, but its combination presents some problems in the case of those 'coming for counselling'. Counsellors argue that these aims are not *necessarily* in conflict and that the professional skill of the social worker lies in their reconciliation and achievement. They are, however, concerned about effectiveness in acting as a safeguard for either applicant or natural mother, and about the boundaries of their work in helping and informing applicants. Counsellors recognise that Section 26 work, interpreted strictly, could be seen 'as a restricted, finite piece of work,' but this goes against their experience; it is 'a failure to see the complexity of dimensions of the thing'.

Counsellors believe that in many cases one interview is insufficient for an adequate assessment of a person's motives or stability: in that sense counselling fails as a safeguard. In the words of one counsellor, 'Even Rampton psychiatrists get it wrong, so what chance have we got?' The use of this analogy suggests a very strong sense both of safeguarding and of the danger against which safeguarding is required. Yet the interview cannot act as a safeguard in the strongest sense: the information about the birth certificate must be given during the interview; it cannot be withheld, no matter how worried the counsellor is about the applicant's future actions. Only three counsellors said they actually wanted the right to withhold that basic birth certificate information, but others recognise the difficulty of their situation in such cases. One or two counsellors resolved it by withholding the authorisation to apply to the court for the name of the placing agency, interpreting the need for their signature as evidence of their approval, which in certain cases they felt they could not give. Most counsellors, however, accepted what one called the 'artificiality' of the counselling situation and make every effort to communicate their concerns to the applicant, but ultimately gave the information. Their strategy then was either to proffer no other help at all, in the hope that applicants would simply be unable to find their natural parents, or preferably to maintain contact with the adoptees and seek gradually to modify their views.

Withholding the birth certificate information is not seen as an appropriate strategy because counsellors are worried about the power and the responsibility that would give them:

> I don't see myself as an authority in this situation. I only see myself as an almost, you might say, a go-between, a local end of the information, to hand it over. I wouldn't see myself as having any rights whatsoever to withhold that information and I don't think I would like to have to make that decision, frankly.

Some counsellors described such power as God-like and involving 'divine responsibilities', but this seems to confuse the authoritative exercise of professional discretion with authoritarian imposition; others thought it would affect the interview itself, changing the tone to one of a trial. The situation might develop, as it is claimed has happened in applications to adopt, where applicants would simply learn the right thing to say and the counsellor would not be able to ascertain their 'true' feelings. Counsellors felt that in the same way as one interview is not really adequate to assess a person's stability, it cannot equally be sufficient grounds for withholding the information. Finally, several counsellors argued that giving this power to the social worker would be to provide a 'cop-out' for the workers, who might be too easily tempted to withhold the information rather than to continue working with the applicant.

Such are the difficulties that can arise when an applicant appears likely to cause damage to someone else. Difficulties also arise in which the applicant could be at risk. This occurs when the counsellor and applicant have decided to trace further information and the files giving the placement details have been located. Although the birth certificate information could be devastating to an applicant, counsellors are rarely able to predict this given the little they know about that person's circumstances. The information on the files, however, is likely to be equally if not more damaging and counsellors will be aware of this beforehand (since almost all read through files before discussing them with the applicant). They have to decide whether or not to impart all, some or none of that information. No guidance is available since it is debatable whether the counsellor should even be in the position of acquiring more information for the applicant. Not only does the legislation state that only one interview is required, it also only allows for the imparting of that information which will enable the applicant to acquire a copy of the original birth certificate. However, the facts that the Regulations enable the applicant also to acquire the name of the placing agency and that the 'Notes for Counsellors' and 'Information for Adopted People' indicate that such information might be available encourages counsellors and applicants alike to hunt it out. The dilemma for the counsellor is even greater in this case since there is no legislative requirement stating what must be given. The distinction is essentially that between information received from the GRO and information gathered by the counsellor. The former can be shared with relative equanimity but dilemmas occur with regard to sharing the latter.

Many counsellors were inclined to give applicants all available information, feeling that any piece might be a vital contribution to the identity for which they are searching. However, several problems arise: the first, and probably most important, is that the information could be very damaging to that person's self-esteem; second, the file could contain information damaging to the natural parents; third, the file was not compiled with a view that the adopted person would read it.

As with the birth certificate information many counsellors did not want the responsibility of withholding even information which could damage the applicant. Included in this category might be facts about a person's neglect or abuse as a baby, or being the result of an incestuous relationship or a mother who was a prostitute. Some counsellors thought it appropriate for the applicant to be given as much information as possible and that to withhold it is again being 'God-like': 'I think people on the whole should be given the decision to decide for themselves what they want really.' Another argument advanced was that if adopted people are given as much information as possible they are less likely to want to trace their natural parent(s). Opinions are not clear-cut on this matter, however, and many counsellors have used their discretion in deciding what information to release. One social worker described her aim as giving as much information as possible 'within the limitations of their capacity to cope with it'. Others 'vet' or 'doctor' files, but do not necessarily tell 'untruths', the aim being to avoid 'deliberately damaging somebody'. Although the preference is to postpone giving information rather than withhold it, withholding does occur since as one counsellor said, social workers are 'agents of social control' as well as 'enablers' and 'helpers'. The information counsellors are most worried about imparting is that which indicates the adoptee was neglected or abused by the natural parents.

A less common worry, but one that also arises in connection with these files, is that of presenting a damaging picture of the natural parents and that of remembering that the files when compiled were assumed to be confidential. In the first case, one or two social workers had to remind themselves that the natural parents had a right to protection and privacy as well, so that some things in their past should perhaps not be spelt out to the applicant. Another counsellor said that he was unhappy about releasing information from local authority files because those files had been written on the assumption that they would be confidential and the people who wrote them were not there to be asked to interpret that information.

Solutions to these problems
Few counsellors believe that the problems outlined above could be solved through tighter legislative action. Solutions are to be found in professional judgement and skill in doing what is appropriate in each particular case. This presents a particularly interesting situation, since the counsellors recognise that in important respects they are not treating applicants as 'clients'. Although the term 'client' is quite frequently employed, its usage is recognised as wrong ('Oh! well they're not clients') or inappropriate ('it shouldn't, but it comes natural to call everybody clients'). Sometimes it seems there simply is no other word, and certainly no regular use was made of the term we have used, applicant. However, in the case of Section 26 work, we have a situation in which social work skills and judgements are explicitly involved in relation to people not easily classified as clients, though they may over time and following an assessment of motivation become explicitly defined as clients in an unqualified way.

The notion of 'professional judgement' is central to most counsellors' view of their role in Section 26 counselling. Their professional judgement, based on the training and skills of social work, is what makes them most suitable for undertaking Section 26 counselling. The 'professional casework training', as they see it, equips them with a range of abilities: to assess applicants to see what is going on 'below the surface'; to relate what is being said to previous experiences; to be aware of what is important to the person; to be able to listen and respond constructively; to be aware of the significance of what is *not* being said; to deal generally with people's feelings in a sensitive manner. Besides these general interviewing skills, counsellors also possess varying degrees of knowledge and experience of adoption, whether as, for example, generic social workers doing guardian *ad litem* reports or as specialist workers assessing applicants to adopt.

One of the most important specific skills they identified in Section 26 counselling was their judgement of time and of pacing. The postponing of certain pieces of information was mentioned several times as a strategy to slow down impetuous or worrying applicants but it is a general principle at work throughout this task. As one counsellor said, 'time is an important tool', and it is a general social work principle to work at the client's pace. This is used particularly when imparting difficult information to the applicant. The counsellor is there to provide information, 'but to be discretionary how they provide that, the timing of it'. The social worker is sensitive to the fact that people need time to take things in and the skill is in assessing how much a person can take at any one time. Counsellors also use their social work skills in judging *what* information to use and their role in interpreting that information. In discussing the imparting of 'nasty' information one counsellor said:

> The other thing one has to be aware of is that if *I* couldn't handle it, how could I expect them to? I would obviously have to prepare *myself* to be very open and honest about it.

Counsellors must

> Measure very carefully how much we say. That maybe if their birth was surrounded by other very terrible happenings, then it might not be helpful to that person to know.

One problem for those counsellors who have easy access to additional information is recognised as the temptation to give too much, too soon: applicants need to get used to the idea of a 'previous' identity with another name and another mother, instead of a 'formless, featureless, nameless image' before they can assimilate other details. The essential thing, according to one counsellor, is 'to be told you are normal': the details can come later.

'Professional judgement' also comes into play in deciding *not* to use social work skills: that is, not to 'social work' people simply because they have applied for this information. In this sense, counselling is distinct from casework because the applicant can very easily set the tone and pace of the interview. According to one social worker counselling by tradition is helping people with a problem, and the problem in Section 26 counselling is defined as 'being adopted', which 'of course isn't a problem', or at least not necessarily a problem. Counsellors believe they should set themselves boundaries in counselling and remember they are dealing with adults, so they can only work with what the applicants give them, rather than delve too much. They will, in consequence, let some things go which they might normally pick up on in a casework interview, unless the applicant specifically indicates a wish to discuss it.

We have seen that counsellors perceive their task in relation to how far along the path to meeting the natural parent any particular applicant wishes to go. Their decision on how much help to give an applicant depends on their assessment of that applicant's motives for making the enquiries and their motivation to pursue them. Behind this assessment is the responsibility social workers as a profession feel for the natural parents, as well as an interpretation of the law which can only make sense of compulsory counselling in terms of the assessment of applicants as a protection for natural parents. In Section 26 the adopted people are the actual social work 'clients' but the natural parents may be viewed as *invisible clients*, the people perhaps for whom the counselling really exists. Because of the need to protect natural parents social workers have devised categories of 'reasonable' and 'unreasonable' motives and motivation. 'Reasonable' motivation is identified as a willingness to pace their assimilation and acquisition of information. Applicants who worry counsellors fail to display this reasonableness and control. These are typically young applicants, those unwilling to talk, and those who display signs of mental instability. Counsellors have to decide in all cases how much extra help to give such applicants in tracing further information and natural parents, and it is their assessment of applicants which is the major influence on their interpretation and application of the legislation in a particular case. Counsellors appear to use at least three counselling strategies to cope with the different assessments of applicants: we have typified these as the 'enabler', the 'detective' and the 'safeguarder'.

The *enabler* is the strategy adopted when counsellors, having given the birth certificate information at the first interview and discussed the implications of searching further with the applicant, make themselves available for further contact and discussion. They will also obtain whatever official records exist but will do no active searching-out of other information on the grounds that the applicant must be sufficiently motivated to do the search alone, thereby ensuring that the search proceeds at the applicant's pace.

The *detective* is similar to the enabler but more *actively* participates in the applicant's search. The 'detective' counsellors will tend to do most of the searching-out of registers and files themselves, partly because they like the work and find it intriguing, but also because continued involvement can provide further protection for all parties affected by the search, making their use as an intermediary more likely.

The *safeguarder* is perhaps the opposite of the detective. This strategy arises when counsellors are concerned by the applicant's motives and motivation that they will try to delay giving them the information and attempt to help them with the perceived problem, rather than immediately with the Section 26 enquiries. If this strategy is not successful, the counsellor has to give the birth information on the applicant's request.

These three categories present an idealisation of what actually occurs, but they convey a sense of the different strategies employed in Section 26 counselling and reflect the range of intepretation placed on the legislation. They are styles which counsellors themselves recognise and confirm. It is important to realise, however, that these styles are not mutually exclusive. Each can be employed by the same counsellor on different occasions with different applicants, and counsellors can switch from one to the other with the same applicant as their relationship develops. There is some evidence to indicate that those with more experience of Section 26 are more inclined to adhere to multiple strategies.

Alfred Leeding (1980), in his study on access to birth records in 1977, found that Section 26 presented counsellors with a dilemma:

> Social workers . . . have found it hard to reconcile the somewhat limited administrative objective with their social work aspirations. Their quandary may be expressed in the words, 'how far do we go?', to which of course there can be no general answer. (p.16)

These three styles of counselling indicate that in the course of practice some general answers have in fact arisen. Leeding's point, however, is not to be ignored, and elsewhere in the same brief but perceptive article he says:

> counselling, in this context, is an amalgam of law and administration on the one hand, and social work practice on the other. It is thus a reflection of the adoption process itself. (p.16)

In the context of Section 26 social work practice and aspirations hinge on the word 'counselling'. Though the considerations of counselling *per se* are accepted as secondary to the purpose of the legislation the ethos of the word does appear to have some influence on their practice in Section 26, and in fact can be seen in each of the three styles. Probably the most commonly preferred strategy, in terms of practical considerations as well as social work principles, is the 'enabler'. This reflects certain key concepts that counsellors associate with 'proper' counselling, even though very few are able to define what counselling is.

Conclusion

Section 26 gave social workers a new group of recipients who could not easily be assimilated into the existing category of 'client'; it also associated a known term, 'counselling', with both the compulsory delivery of certain information and with compulsory attendance at a counselling session. Counsellors say that they spend little time considering these conceptual conflicts, but as they describe their problems in responding appropriately to situations, it is clear that they implicitly sense them. In addition, they interpret any general problems in the light of their past professional experience and their cumulative experience of Section 26 work. As the problems and their operational solutions unfold and are recognised we can see not only the making of a new service in adoption (and, as we shall see later, a potential new service for all children in long-term care away from their natural families), but also behaviour more generally characteristic of social work professionals. Observing how those called social workers and those acknowledging themselves as such define and solve problems in one area of practice casts much more light on the nature of social work than any lengthy discussion of general definitions.

5 The Consumer Perspective

Introduction

This chapter examines applicants' use and opinion of the legislation. The following chapter sets this within the wider context of their general experience of being adopted. It will become apparent that a sociological perspective on the 'adoptive experience' is as revealing in the case of individuals as it is in the case of organisations. Our analysis and subsequent treatment of data from the applicants has led us to question concepts used in earlier studies of tracing information and natural parents.

One of the most common assumptions, held by researchers and practitioners alike, is that there is a strong relationship between the quality of the adoptive experience and the desire to trace natural parents – the poorer the former, the stronger the latter. (See, for example, Triseliotis, 1973.) We have found that this wish to correct present relationships by tracing natural parents is only one feature in the process, and one which unduly emphasises the psycho-pathological image of the adopted person. Instead, we argue for a social and, more specifically, an inter-actional perspective on tracing and on adoption as a whole. This leads us to suggest that instead of a picture of adoptees as 'psychological vagrants' rushing around looking for a new set of family relationships, a more rational picture is available: that is, of adoptees seeking to place themselves socially, in order to remove the unease they and others feel about their adoptive status. We shall argue that adopted persons who make enquiries, privately as well as publicly through Section 26, are seeking to correct their marginal status. What has often been described in simple terms as the adopted person's search for a sense of identity can be more fully understood as a desire for the *ability* to ask, without censure, about one's story and to ask others about their part in one's story. Adoptees are seeking to place themselves in a narrative, and they do this in order to correct that part of their lives which gives them a marginal identity, that is, their ignorance about certain key people and events in their lives.

To be the subject of a narrative that runs from one's birth to one's death is . . . to be accountable for the actions and experiences which compose a narratable life. It is . . . to be open to being asked to give a certain kind of account of what one did or what happened to one or what one witnessed at any earlier point in one's life . . . The other aspect of narrative selfhood is correlative: I am not only accountable, I am one who can always ask others for an account, who can put others to the question. I am part of their story as they are part of mine. The narrative of any one life is part of an interlocking set of narratives. Moreover this asking for and giving of accounts itself plays an important part in constituting narratives. Asking what you did and why, saying what I did and why, pondering the differences between your account of what I did and my account of what I did, and vice versa, these are essential constituents of all but the very simplest and barest of narratives. (MacIntyre 1981: 202-3)

The use of Section 26 can be seen as a specific example of a request for an account. As such it is a 'public' request and, after examining the details of the process and the issues it raises, we shall locate it within the allegedly 'private' sphere of adoptive family life.

The context of enquiries

Most adopted people interviewed for the research had made other enquiries before applying under Section 26. For most these consisted of intra-familial questions and discussions which were both limited and difficult. A few respondents had actually reached their original placing agency, but again felt they were not being told everything there was to know. Their use of Section 26 should be viewed within the context of these other enquiries. There was, however, a qualitative difference to this particular course of action, most especially its public nature. Many of their previous enquiries had been secretive, individual and fragmentary. Here was a procedure legally, and hence socially sanctioned, providing information to which they now had a right. Whilst it did not remove all secrecy, since the majority did not tell their adoptive parents they were applying, it did remove some of the shame.

Most adopted people heard about the law through the media, whose coverage tended to emphasise the more sensational aspects, particularly that of actual reunions between adoptees and natural parents. This helps to explain the expectations that some applicants had of the law; that it was not simply a matter of access to birth records but of finding out everything there was to know about their natural parents: 'I interpreted this as I can find out who my father was, where he lived, where he worked, what he was, what size shoe he takes, everything.'

For the majority of applicants using Section 26 was seen as a significant step but they were not sure where it would take them. A certain amount of hesitation was evident, springing from a desire to protect not only their adoptive parents but also themselves:

> It was a while after it came out that I decided to do it. I felt that I had to be sure in myself that I wanted to do it. I think if you're unsure it's not worth doing it. I think it's something you've got to be really *positive* about, that you can face like both sides of the thing: if you cannot find her or you *do* find her and she doesn't want to know you.

Applicants varied widely in what they wanted to know, and this suggests that most did not realise the legislative limits on the information they could receive under Section 26. It also indicates that Section 26 was part of their general enquiries which for many had no clearly articulated goal. The sort of questions they were asking themselves and others were: Who am I? Why was I adopted? What were the circumstances of my birth? Where was I born? What was my original name? What sort of life might I have had? Other aims included wishing to confirm what they felt they already knew and wanting a copy of their original birth certificate. Every applicant wanted at least one of these things, and most wanted a combination of all or several. At least 16 of the 45 applicants interviewed felt they wanted this sort of information but were not sure how much, or quite how far they wished to take their enquiries. Another 23 wanted information but felt they also wanted to trace a natural relative. Four applicants said their main intention was to acquire a copy of their original birth certificate both to confirm what they had already been told and for the sake of having their own copy; one applicant was adamant he merely wanted to confirm that his natural mother was the person he thought she was and that he had no intention of taking his enquiries further; another applicant said her motivation was to acquire medical information and nothing else.

Although almost all applicants who wanted to trace a natural relative focused their attention on their natural mother, this was sometimes only a matter of expediency. Several applicants were more interested in meeting siblings or the natural father and thought of the natural mother as the only available source of information. Others wanted to know about both parents but tended to be pessimistic about their chances of finding out anything about the father: 'I know I'm going to come up against a brick wall as far as my father is concerned and that really is as important to me as my mother.'

Despite the various specific goals individuals wanted to achieve, two general features were present in most accounts of why Section 26 had been used. One of these was the difficulty they experienced in expressing satisfactorily the reasons for their enquiry:

> at the time I kept thinking it was just out of curiosity and that did not seem the right answer. I kept thinking, I says 'I don't know, I think I'm just curious', and yet that wasn't the answer I wanted to put over; I just couldn't think of the reason, probably just to know. I still don't know to this day, except I'd just like to know.

Something so self-evidently reasonable as, say, wanting to know who your parents are becomes immediately complex when needing explanation. This lack of an available script indicates the unusual nature of the quest and leads to the second feature of applicants' accounts, which we have labelled 'just-talk'. Applicants use the word 'just' to normalise their request, thus minimising its dramatic and, therefore, potentially threatening nature: 'I just wanted to find out who I was basically'; 'I just wanted to find out who my mother and father were'; 'It was just curiosity over the name'. Similarly, applicants were keen to express their natural (as opposed to morbid or idle) curiosity and to avoid any image of themselves as being obsessed or out of control. 'I used to wonder, naturally you do, but I never had a sort of obsession that I know some people have when they know that they're adopted, to find out their parents.'

The expectations and experience of the counselling service

Awareness of how their enquiries might be seen by others provided applicants with an explanation of why *compulsory* counselling was a requirement for receiving the information:

> I assumed it would be some sort of a test and if you weren't thought suitable to be allowed to have the information you would

not be given it. I wasn't otherwise certain what the function of the counsellor was supposed to be.

The idea of compulsory counselling could not, of course, have actually deterred any of those interviewed, but they could imagine how others might be. This could be for practical reasons:

> I must admit I thought God, you know. Oh, I mean it's enough really to put you off, isn't it? It's going through all the rig-marole . . . I'm sure if somebody was working full-time and they had to take a half-day's leave or whatever, I'm sure it would actually put them off.

Alternatively, it might arise from a sense of vulnerability,

> I don't know really what I expected but it all seemed a bit daunting, all a bit official and I think it's the word 'counselling' that sort of, you know, made me wonder, sounds a bit like the third degree . . .

Very few applicants had had previous experience of social workers and were unsure what to expect. Generally the image was poor; one applicant said he thought social workers were 'out of touch with reality, weirdos'. Another claimed, 'I have always found them to be very poor, totally inexperienced, people.' However, the reality of the counsellor was in most cases quite different from the expectation:

> I thought she'd be all posh an' all, you know, like they are sometimes, sit behind a desk. But she wasn't. I sat beside her and had a smoke with her, and things like that. You know, it was good.

Just as social workers were pleasantly surprised by the reality of the applicants under Section 26, so applicants were surprised by the helpful reality of the social workers. Applicants were impressed by the amount of time counsellors were prepared to spend with them, and with their general demeanour. Older applicants were glad the counsellors tended to be mature because they thought them experienced in the matters being discussed, and in a position of authority. They felt that not only could they trust the counsellor's judgement and opinions but also that the counsellor would be able to acquire more information by exercising that authority.

Applicants fell into two groups in terms of the duration and, to some extent, the content of the counselling: for the majority the interview lasted between 30 minutes and an hour, but a few said that the first interview only lasted 15 to 20 minutes. The difference appears to lie in the detail in which the applicant's past experiences and future intentions were discussed, and this of course required a willingness on both parties to enter into an extended discussion. One group of applicants who all had the same counsellor tended to have fairly long first interviews of about an hour. One of these described the content of his interview by saying, 'there was a build-up to counselling' in which the counsellor asked him about his background, his thoughts on adoption, his relationship with his adoptive parents and how he knew he was adopted. He found it easy to talk to the counsellor because she was 'leading' him. Another man who had the same counsellor said 'she went around the town' to explain things to him which he found useful because he could remember what she said more easily. He felt relaxed and said the discussion 'wandered off the track' and then went back to the reasons for his application. This applicant, like several others, remembered stories the counsellor told of other adoptees searching, and these served to illustrate both the dangers and the benefits of what they were doing. A slightly different approach was described by another applicant who said her counsellor just asked her what she already knew, then disclosed her original name and her natural mother's name and only then discussed the possibilities of tracing and the dangers of so doing. Several applicants compared the counselling interview with the research interview: 'It was a bit like chatting to you now. We just sort of talked over what I did know and why did I want my birth certificate.'

A smaller group of applicants remembered their counselling as very much briefer. They attributed this to the fact that the counsellor could clearly see they represented no danger to anyone and could be trusted to handle the information carefully. One applicant said his counsellor asked the same 'preliminary questions' as the research interviewer, in order to start him talking so that she could then assess his motives. Another thought that his counsellor did not need to stress the 'delicateness of the subject' since she could 'obviously' tell he would not go 'crashing in'. In the words of another applicant: 'I think she realised I was pretty sensible.'

Most applicants were aware not only of what was said, but also how and why it was said. The experience of counselling confirmed their expectations, which, whether it lasted 10 minutes or an hour, was to 'weigh them up', to assess their motivation and their ability to cope with what they were doing before the information was imparted. They felt that the tactic employed for doing this was to posit all the possible dangers and pitfalls of acquiring information: 'The counsellor really put all the stumbling-blocks in front of me . . . not trying to put me off but showing me all what could happen.' Even those who had no intention of trying to trace natural parents felt this: one man, who had already met his natural mother prior to counselling and simply wanted more information, considered the first counselling session as crucial because the social worker made him aware of what 'the road to information' might be like. He felt that the fact that he made it clear to her that he was prepared for that made her more open with him.

Applicants had mixed reactions to this strategy, however. Some felt the counsellors were being realistic and helping them to realise the limitations on what could be achieved, whereas others felt that they were deliberately trying to put them off finding out more information. Few applicants had specific comments or complaints about particular features of the counselling, although one woman was very annoyed that the counsellor had her file but would not let her see it herself: 'I thought I had a right to see it . . . she read out bits of this and bits of that and . . . it was a case of, if you don't remember it, too bad.' This made her wonder what was on the file that the counsellor did not wish her to see.

In summary, applicants were glad the counsellor was friendly, they could appreciate the techniques employed but ultimately their assessment of the counselling and of the legislation as a whole centred on the amount of information they received. According to the letter of the law the only information that should be imparted in the first interview is the applicant's original name, the natural mother's name and, if known, the natural father's name. In fact nearly half those interviewed (21 out of 45) already knew the first two pieces of information, so strictly speaking they had no need to apply through Section 26 for a copy of their birth certificate. That they did so perhaps indicates that they did not know the detailed form of the law. On the other hand, seeing this information written down somehow made it more 'real' for them. 'I wanted an identity, you know. Oh, once I got my name I was thrilled to bits. In fact I was all for changing it there and then.' Although this applicant did not formally change her name, she used her original Christian name in her new job: 'I'm getting called by my *proper* name now.' These applicants associated their name, more than any other piece of information, with what they considered to be the essence of their identity although they found it difficult to articulate the connection: 'and your mind goes blank, you can't explain it at all, it's just an alien name completely . . . and it's me.' In contrast to this reaction another woman had expected her original name to be similarly important as part of her search for an identity: 'It's who you *are*, yes, that's it. "Who am I?" And when I did find out my name it didn't make a damn bit of difference.'

Simply knowing their natural parents' names had little impact on most applicants unless, as in one case, the name was already known to them. The name did, however, serve to personify the people involved. The impact of this tended to be negative if the adoptee had expected to recognise the name. One man described a feeling of anti-climax, 'because there's always these fantasies about being the Duke of Northumberland's son or something'. Discovering the place of their birth often had a greater impact since, as one male applicant mentioned, it felt very odd to discover he had been born in a place he thought he had never even visited before. Similarly, one woman felt strange on hearing her natural father had been Polish, 'because I had always considered myself wholly British before'. New knowledge such as this involves an immediate rearranging of the facts of the individual's life, and a 're-placing' in a new biography.

Post-counselling activities

Once applicants have received at least the basic birth certificate information from the counsellor they have to decide what to do with it: should they simply store it away or use it to trace further information or natural parents? For some the decision had apparently already been made; it was contained in their reason for applying for this information in the first place. These applicants fell into two groups: those with a clear intention to trace a member or members of their natural family (23 applicants) and those who had set a clear limit on the extent of their enquiries (6 applicants). The remaining 16 were unsure of what they wanted. However, the number of applicants who eventually tried to trace their natural parents rose to at least 28: the change of goals occurred in each direction; 2 applicants who initially wanted to trace their parents decided not to; 6 applicants who were originally unsure of their intentions resolved their indecision, 5 by attempting to trace parents and one by deciding he had found out as much information as he wanted: 2 applicants who had set firm limits on what they wanted to know decided in the end to attempt to trace members of their original families.

It is evident from these figures that the decision over what to do and how far to go, is extremely difficult and fraught with emotional and practical problems. These problems will be discussed in more detail in the following chapter, but our concerns here are with the continued relationship, or lack of it, between applicant and counsellor and how this influenced the applicant's actions.

For those who decided to find out more information various avenues could be explored. From the counsellor they each had the authority to apply to the court for the name of the agency that placed them for adoption; they could use the birth certificate to see if their natural mother still lived at the same address; they could use the registers in London to see if their mother had married or died or had other children; they could even make enquiries through knowing their mother's (and perhaps father's) occupation. Any or all of these steps could be taken with or without the guidance and advice of the counsellor.

Just over half the applicants saw their counsellor more than once, the counsellor being the source of more detailed information and/or advice as to other sources. The counsellor often applied to the court on the applicant's behalf and would then contact the placing agency to request their records. Alternatively, those applicants who were placed by the authority in which they were counselled had even easier access to information, unless the records had been lost or destroyed. If this had happened the only source of information was the birth certificate and, in rare instances, the copy of the guardian *ad litem* report released by the court. The lack of records and the failure to find information from alternative sources, effectively put an end to the search in several cases. It did not diminish the desire for information or the desire to meet the natural parents, but the applicants in question were not prepared to follow up the one source of information available to them: their adoptive families.

Many of the applicants whose records were extant were pleasantly surprised by the amount of information they received from the counsellor. This consisted in many cases not just of dates and other bare facts but also information about why the applicants had been placed for adoption, as well as in one man's words, 'an idea of what the system was all about'. The information enabled them to understand both the general circumstances at the time of their placement as well as the particular circumstances of their natural mother's position. As one applicant said, knowing *why* things happen, 'fills things out more in your mind. You feel more sympathetic.' The files from the placing agencies often contained letters and photographs indicating in many cases that the natural mother had tried to look after the adoptee before finally relinquishing the child for adoption. Adoptees were glad to know this because it resolved some of their feelings of rejection. One applicant, however, expressed the mixed feelings that arose when he was given a photograph of himself with his natural mother: he realised that having him had not been a totally bad experience for his mother, but on the other hand, he felt some anger and wondered if she had really tried hard enough to keep him. The mixed feelings expressed by this applicant were the source of his uncertainty whether to take his enquiries further or not. As with several other applicants he decided to defer the decision about meeting until that was actually possible and meanwhile to continue tracing names and addresses until he found his natural mother's whereabouts.

This was the next step for those applicants who, having discovered the circumstances of their adoption, wanted to find current information, either because they wanted to trace parents or because they had not yet decided. At this stage, in most cases, counsellors were not much direct practical help to applicants because their information was from the time of placement.

For some applicants the activity of seeking information became satisfying for its own sake and they found that the more information they obtained the more they wanted. They enjoyed the search and became more intrigued concerning the person about whom they were collecting information. As they got closer in their search to their mother's current whereabouts the more logical it seemed actually to attempt to meet her. As one man said, 'I was completely hooked on it, if you like', and although the original intention was simply to find out information in the end he wanted to meet her. This happened in at least seven cases, where applicants who had been unsure of their original intentions or who had only wanted limited information discovered in the course of their investigations that they did want to meet their natural parent(s) after all. However, one applicant also decided that, when he got as far as finding someone with his natural father's name who was married, he had taken his enquiries far enough. He felt he did not have so great a need to know anything more that it was worth disturbing someone.

In contrast to this group of applicants who appeared to have exhausted every line of enquiry was a small group of about five applicants who had very little success, mostly because they felt lost in their search for information. Some of these were applicants who had expected more help from the counsellors in tracing their parents and when this was not forthcoming, for whatever reason, they did not know where to start looking:

> The woman [the counsellor] was amazingly sympathetic, really wishing me luck and meaning it, but I sort of walked out a little confused, feeling great, you know, but not knowing where I was going or what I was going to do next. I mean I had all the luck in the world and handshakes and all that, but I still walked out of there as bloody ignorant as when I walked in. I didn't know what to do next, so I sort of gave up on it a little bit.

Several of these applicants had tried making some enquiries, but had not followed up every lead open to them: others had not even made basic enquiries from registers and electoral rolls. Although each still wanted more information and possibly to trace, it appears that they were being held back not just by ignorance but also, in two cases at least, by a lack of anyone to help them in their search and the fearfulness, expressed by others, of what they might find out.

Most applicants who succeeded in tracing natural parents did so with the help of one or several counsellors, over and above the initial interview. Even if the tracing was done mostly by themselves several applicants used the counsellor to make the first contact with the natural parent.

> Yes, we went back for advice. We knew we had the information there. 'OK, let's be responsible, we'll go back, we'll lay the information down and she'll tell us then the best way of going about it,' which she did. We knew we were definitely not going to go knocking on the door, that was definite . . .

There was a strong sense that this was not only the responsible thing to do, in order to give the natural parent the chance to refuse to meet, but that it was also the 'proper' thing to do.

One applicant who failed to receive what she deemed appropriate help from her counsellor was left to make enquiries on her own, 'which was the way I didn't really want to do it. I thought it was, you know, secretive and not right. I would prefer it was done properly, through a counsellor.'

Assessment of the service

This last comment illustrates one of the key features of the legislation as far as applicants are concerned; it provides public approval of their enquiries. Added emphasis is given to this approval by the fact of its delivery through someone deemed by applicants to be a professional, who appears to know all the issues, and who *still* in most cases approves. As one applicant said,

> Well, I felt I had somebody on my side. . . . She knew what I wanted and she was prepared to help, where all sorts of relatives and everybody else didn't want to help. . . . She knew exactly where to get this information from, that I hadn't a clue where to start looking.

On this level little distinction is made between the legislation as a whole and the compulsory counselling. However, as we have seen, another key feature in the appreciation of the legislation as far as the applicants are concerned is the amount of information available. This was where most disappointment and even bitter frustration was expressed:

> I've been passed from [the counsellor] to the courts, from the courts to the Registrar, from the Registrar back to [the counsellor]. . . . I'm getting the buck passed. That's where I am at the moment: I've got the joke, I want the punchline.

At least one person felt the information was available but was being withheld simply because of who he was and the status of his enquiries: 'Well, I mean, if the police wanted her they'd find her like that [clicking fingers]. But I can't, can I? I resent that a little bit.'

Most applicants approved of compulsory counselling, reiterating their feeling of it as a test, but also incidentally underlining the essentially reasonable nature of their own enquiries in the face of potential distrust.

> Not everybody's like me. A lot of people could get very uptight – maybe they have the wrong reasons for trying to find out, that's why as the laws stands, I think it's good.

Some applicants felt that the actual experience of counselling did have an effect on them, most commonly a 'calming' influence. Others felt the pacing of the procedure gave them time to think:

I certainly expected to fill in a few forms, but I think from when you first start out, I think that the time it takes you to find out . . . you need that little bit of time really, rather than sort of rushing into things. For all that I had thought about it beforehand I was still thinking, 'Oh, it would be great', you know, 'get on like a house of fire.' It just gave me time to realise that it might not just turn out that way.

Those few applicants who did object to the compulsory counselling tended to be resigned to it, even though one described it as 'a bit of paternalistic nonsense'.

Few, if any, applicants had any doubts about the appropriateness of access to birth records, even though they expressed due caution on behalf of both natural and adoptive parents.

Two comments convey the predominant opinions about the aspects of the legislation that affected applicants most. First the counselling:

Counselling to me meant a straightforward case of this is where you stand inside the law – this is what you can do, this is what you can't do; these are the fringe areas, don't mess about too greatly in them, sort of attitude . . . a straightforward commonsense approach.

and the counsellors:

She was good, she really wanted to know if I found her. I was well impressed with her. Oh yes, the social worker was a true blue social worker, she cared like, you know. She would have given me a bowl of soup, you know, if she had a chance, but she was all right.

6   The Adoptive Experience

A narrative sense of self

The use of Section 26, as with other enquiries adult adoptees make about their origins, is part of the adoptive experience and can be better understood in this wider context. One aspect of that experience which Section 26 highlights is the loss of certain features of the adoptees' lives, such as their natural parents, their original name, the knowledge of why they were adopted, knowledge of their early physical appearance, and so on. These features have been removed and some of them replaced. Writers who have previously explored the effect of this on adoptees have emphasised the psychopathological aspects, and talked of the necessity for the adoptee to undergo a period of grief and mourning for the past (see, for example, Triseliotis 1976). Shawyer has even spoken of the adoptee's 'death by adoption'.

We would like to suggest another dimension which looks at the impact on the adoptees' social world and hence on their social, as opposed to ego, identity. On the most prosaic level, adopted people, lacking these pieces of information, are vulnerable simply because they cannot recount with confidence their own full life-history. Examples which are at the very least embarrassing recur frequently in adoptees' accounts of their past, such as being unable to help a child with a family tree, to produce a birth certificate for a job interview, to satisfy prospective in-laws about their background. On other occasions this lack of knowledge is not merely embarrassing but is positively dangerous, and adoptees feel all the more foolish for that: the lack of a medical history during pregnancy is commonly quoted. A narrative sense of self is important in all aspects of life, as Barbara Hardy (1968) points out:

> we dream in narrative, daydream in narrative, remember, anticipate, hope, despair, believe, doubt, plan, revise, criticise, construct, gossip, learn, hate and love by narrative. In order really to live we make up stories about ourselves and others, about the personal as well as the social past and future. . . .

The difficulty for adoptees is that not only may such daydreams be dismissed as 'fantasies' but that there is very little certain knowledge available about their origins. A second difficulty particular to adoptees is that as well as having such gaps in their knowledge as we all do, their attempts to fill those gaps are met with censure, some of it self-imposed.

This chapter will look at the way that lack of knowledge is, and has been, sustained and the difficulties adoptees face in trying to correct it. We shall see how those who have succeeded in doing so talk about the effect this has had on their sense of identity. One adoptee sums up the dilemma each faces:

> I've thought about [tracing my natural parents] as the only method of finding out. I mean it's a very difficult or very hard decision to make about that but I suppose as I get older I realise more and more life is such an extraordinary thing in what happens to one, it's terrible not having a part of one's story, it's very hard to account for the way one is.

Telling and knowing: intra-familial aspects of adoption

A certain lack of knowledge has been sustained publicly, through the confidentiality of adoption registration and agency records, and privately, within the family. However optimistic practitioners may be about current and future practice in adoption, those adults currently using Section 26 have suffered these dual pressures of secrecy in keeping them ignorant about certain aspects of their past. The feature of adoption that is usually described as 'telling' highlights the intra-familial problems.

There are at least two ways of gaining the knowledge of one's adoptive status: either by being told by one's adoptive parents or by finding out from some other source, such as neighbours, overhearing a conversation, looking secretly through family papers, and so on. Two-thirds of our sample had in fact been told by the adoptive parents, and this could at first sight be taken as a positive sign of the increasing openness of adoption, especially as the timing of the telling was such that one-third felt they had 'always known' they were adopted. Early telling is usually seen as 'good' telling by practitioners. Few acquired the knowledge through the medium of the family row much loved by fiction writers. However, for this group of applicants knowledge of their status did not always mean they understood the significance of the fact and, when understanding dawned, it was almost like a second 'telling', as one applicant recalled:

And it just suddenly dawned on me that it was real, it was for real. But I don't think I really knew *then* quite what adoption meant. I'd had this thing drummed into me, year after year, but still didn't know what it really meant.

Some adopted people suspect their status before being formally told, and their understanding of its significance, as well as the extra time they have had to reflect upon it, appear to mitigate the possible shock that some adoptees report, arising less from the late telling as such and more from the immediate realisation of its significance. As Goffman (1963) says, 'The painfulness then . . . can come not from the individual's confusion about his identity, but from knowing too well what he has become' (p. 158).

The older adoptee can also suffer stress from a 'late telling', not so much from the fact of adoption as from the method of discovery:

I found out from somebody who lived opposite, not from my own parents. There was a girl opposite who also was adopted and her adoptive parents told her and of course she was very upset, so to soften the blow they said, 'Well, of course, you know X is adopted too,' and she came straight out and told me, and I didn't know anything about it till then and I went home and I was so upset, more because I'd been told that way, you know.

The gaining of this knowledge, however and wherever it occurs, cannot fail to affect the subsequent relationship between parent and adoptee. Inevitably the adoptee is immediately curious to know more, but very rarely is this curiosity easily satisfied. Even those who have 'always known' they were adopted appeared, in fact, to know very little of the surrounding details. As young children they may have asked questions 'without realising', as one man put it, but as they gradually got older and became 'more conscious of relationships', the subject became taboo. 'You never wanted to raise it for fear of upsetting them, I suppose.' The situation was even more difficult for those adoptees who knew of their status, without their parents' knowledge. One applicant, when asked if she had ever questioned her parents directly about her adoption replied,

No I never, it's funny, I never could bring myself to, actually. I think I was a bit frightened what I would find out, you know, I didn't want to believe it, to be honest. . . . I was sort of quite happy as I was.

Sometimes, even when parents did raise the subject, often somewhat tentatively, adoptees refused to take up the subject themselves. We do not, therefore, share Leeding's apparent surprise when he says of Section 26 applicants:

> One or two even went so far as to say that they themselves had contributed to the fiction by being too reserved or sensitive to speak frankly within the family circle. All too often the moment passed, the opportunity for honesty was gone: so the blame is shared. (1980: 12)

Accounts are not easily asked for nor easily given. What appears to be created in many adoptive families is what Glaser and Strauss (1965), in the context of terminal illnesses, have called a 'mutual pretence awareness context'. That is, the fiction of the 'ordinary family' is maintained by the refusal of either party to admit openly to each other the facts that they both know, and that they each know the other knows. Or, as one counsellor put it, adoption is like an elephant in the corner of the sitting-room which everyone affects not to notice.

'Telling', then, is a more complex concept than has perhaps previously been appreciated. In fact, we prefer to use the term 'disclosure' for several reasons: as a new term in this context it has the impact of requiring a new appraisal, a re-examination. Such a review will, we believe, show other features, such as the fact that disclosure occurs over time and is a two-way interactional process. In other words, disclosure, unlike 'telling', is not a one-off, parent-to-adoptee communication, nor even a one-way communication occurring over time, with more details being added. This can occur, of course, but equally the adoptee's role can be and often is more active, so that for example disclosure-to-self can occur, comprising several stages such as suspicion–discovery–confirmation (through telling or self-realisation). All of this without the active involvement of the adoptive parents. Consequently, the *failure* to 'tell' cannot be laid simply at the adoptive parents' feet, since, as we have seen, adoptees themselves participate in the pretence. Therefore, despite the fact that many adoptees appear to know several facts about their pre-adoption past this is generally information gained in a disjointed way, at a fairly young age. Some sort of narrative might be available but they were not always confident of its accuracy: 'the stories were so varied and so far apart, it was impossible to even form an outline, never mind a picture of a person.'

Given their acknowledged complicity in the closed nature of their adoptive family life it is difficult to assess the quality of the applicants' adoptive experiences. Certainly few of them appear to have had unhappy adoptions and it was the wish to preserve their relationship with their adoptive parents which led many of them to make enquiries elsewhere. One obvious source, certainly before the 1975 Children Act, was the wider adoptive family but few met with any satisfactory response. Either the stories given were varied and conflicting or, worse, the initial request was greeted with hostility. For some adoptees the possibility of approaching the wider family was never countenanced since they had never felt a part of that family: 'You know, I wasn't a blood relation and blood counts in families – they never accepted me.' This is an example of what Kirk (1964) describes as the 'achieved' (or failure to be achieved) role of the adoptee as opposed to the 'ascribed' role of the natural child.

Extra-familial enquiries

If adoptees are determined to fill the gaps in their knowledge they are forced eventually to step out of the private sphere of familial enquiries into the public domain of agency records, and even in one case court applications for the release of information. This transition is important not just for the public notification of personal desires but also for the necessity, perhaps for the first time, to *explain* those desires. For some the transition was made easier by their adopters' suggestion that they should perhaps make their enquiries through a third party either because the parents simply did not know the relevant information or because they felt unable to face the experience of telling the adoptee themselves. For most, the placing agency was an obvious source of information, but was found to be equally unforthcoming: 'they were friendly enough but rather reserved and only giving me the information which they felt I ought to have.' Another applicant felt he was clearly being deterred from any attempt to pursue his enquiries further:

I actually didn't like the things the person at the adoption agency said at all and left me feeling very angry about their attitude. They seemed very keen to justify their activities and talked about virtually nothing except money and social status. I mean they seemed entirely concerned, you know, with the whole business of how much better off all those children were, not being looked after by their natural parents, which, perhaps, but questionable.

Other adoptees were met with a total refusal to reveal information or give help in their search. One man, though he was very unusual in this, tried to gain access to his birth records in the only legally-sanctioned process to exist before Section 26, an application through the courts: he was refused access. Several others tried the Salvation Army but were told that their Missing Persons Bureau could not or would not handle adoption cases: 'they said, of course, you know, they couldn't.' Others met a similar reaction from newspapers who ran 'Where are you now?' columns. The applicants themselves appeared not to be surprised by such reactions and accepted that individuals and organisations might be reluctant to release information. As one man said, people's first response to being asked a question might be, 'Am I giving information away that I shouldn't?'. They see adoption as being rife with secrecy and to a certain extent they accept this and even condone it.

Section 26, as we have noted, gave public and therefore social approval to adoptees' curiosity and this, for some applicants, was a welcome justification for their enquiries. However, for many applicants the public/private divide still existed, in as much as they felt unable to tell their adoptive parents that they had made enquiries elsewhere, even after the 1975 Act had been passed. Social approval did not lead to an end to secrecy. For some adoptees the death of an adoptive parent meant that enquiries could be made for the first time: 'when she died I thought, "Well, now I can't upset her, so now I shall try to find out." ' Most simply did not tell their adoptive parents, for fear of hurting them through a sense of betrayal or of not being loved:

> I mean, she doesn't know I've got my original birth certificate, you know. I couldn't tell her anything like that because she would think she was not loved as much. You know, it would be a slight on her.

There is a great similarity between the reasons given by adoptive parents for not informing their child of the adoption and the reasons given by adoptees for not informing their adopters about the enquiries. Secrecy in adoption is maintained by all those involved, not just the adopters.

Pressures against tracing

The wish to protect adoptive parents becomes even stronger when applicants considered whether or not to go so far as attempting to trace natural parents. We have seen some of the practical problems of so doing, but the emotional ones are just as strong. Those who would like very much to trace their parents see their search as fraught with difficulties, and for those who are unsure of their aims the difficulties are perhaps, at that particular time in their lives, more overwhelming than the perceived benefits of tracing natural parents. To an extent a decision to uncover more information represents a decision to defer making a decision about tracing. At some point, however, the seeking-out of information becomes, for some at least, a seeking-out of parents.

Time is an important factor in each applicant's search, particularly for those uncertain of what they want: several have returned to see a counsellor or their agency after one of several long breaks as they have decided they wanted to take their enquiries further each time. The general point to make is that virtually all the applicants in this study have at one time or another considered the possibility of tracing their natural parents: some have dismissed it absolutely; others have been unsure that that is the answer to the questions they are asking; yet others feel that this is what they want to do, whatever the difficulties.

Secrecy relieved them of possibly hurting their parents but not of feelings of guilt at the deceit they considered they were perpetrating. Many lived in fear of their parents finding out and this created practical difficulties in arranging to meet the counsellor and research interviewer, as well as in being able to get on with their enquiries. In every case where applicants informed their parents of their enquiries the parents were upset. In one case, although the applicant had since resumed her enquiries, the effect of telling her adoptive father was such that she stopped temporarily and could not now tell him she had resumed.

> Then two years ago mother died and I felt terrible. I told my dad what I'd been doing and he said, 'I'm glad your mother's not alive to know this.' And the guilt was terrible. I think that was worse than her dying, you know, knowing what I'd done.

The other party applicants were afraid of hurting through their enquiries was their natural parent(s). Most were aware that these parents might have since married and not told their spouses about the child they had placed for adoption or, in the case of fathers, might not even know they had a child. Even if the spouses and children knew of the child in the past, the effect of that child, now adult, entering their present lives might be too traumatic for the parent to manage. Applicants expressed an awareness of the 'delicacy' of tracing a parent, but to a certain extent resolved the problem by saying they would respect their parents' privacy if they refused to meet them.

In terms of making a decision on the extent of their investigations the difficulties associated with the natural parents were caught up with fears applicants had over the damage they could do to themselves. Some applicants feared the disappointment they would incur either through being unable to find any information or through being unable, after successful tracing, to meet a parent. The fear of rejection was and is perhaps the strongest of applicants' fears. On one level they can understand the natural parent's wish not to be disturbed, but on another it would serve to confirm a feeling of having been rejected at time of birth:

> I would respect her wishes. I'm not saying it wouldn't hurt if she said, 'I don't want to know, I don't want to meet her.' It *would* hurt, it's obvious, I'm sort of being rejected again, but it's something you'd have to get over.

The reasons people gave for wanting to trace were no different from those given for wanting information in general, other than the additional impact of actually seeing the parent. 'Just-talk' was as evident in tracers and non-tracers alike. For those who decided not to trace, or who were unable to do so, positive benefits were still derived from simply getting the birth certificate. One woman said she felt:

> relieved, I think, that I was a person. I just thought I wasn't even counted as a person . . . you just sort of feel a nobody, 'til I got this information. That's my name and that's where I was born – the *truth*, there's no lies behind it.

The impact of what Manning (1972) calls a 'paper identity' should not be underestimated, especially for those applicants who simply wanted a birth certificate and nothing else. It is as though 'The person's body assumes the property of a mere *appearance*, verifying the need for a permanent and real record of his organisational existence' (Manning 1972).

In contrast, for those going on to trace, the parents' physical appearance was, or became, more important. The physical similarity between themselves and their parents was one of the first things they noticed when meeting.

> I sort of went into the room and there my mother was, standing there – it was very emotional. We both cried buckets and buckets, but the first thing I can remember thinking about was, was I like her? That this was her – I could see myself in her straight away.

Having had a first meeting not everyone sustained the relationship with a natural parent, either because meeting once and acquiring information was enough to satisfy them, or because practical difficulties made contact difficult. For those who did sustain a relationship, problems still existed. The decision over whether or not to tell adoptive parents was one, but the natural parents also had to decide whether or not to tell their families. Spouses were easier to inform than subsequent children, so the adoptee often became a 'family friend', as far as the latter were concerned.

Effect of the search

We have seen that there are multiple possible outcomes to an attempt by adoptees to trace information and/or natural parents: they can give up from a lack of information or out of consideration for self, adoptive and natural parents; they may succeed in tracing but decline to meet or be refused such a meeting; a meeting can take place and then contact dropped; or a sustained relationship can occur. We have seen also that those who have been forced to give up through lack of information or, indeed, who are still trying, experience a sense of frustration and even anger at what they interpret as attempts to prevent them pursuing their intentions. What about those, however, who have succeeded in their enquiries, who have gone as far as they want and achieved all the information and contact they desire: how do they talk about the meaning their search has had for them? A general feature of their talk is a feeling of knowing, of completion, of certainty:

> It just confirms – it gives you a little bit more of an identity. It's very hard to explain. I'm not the sort of person that really *cares* what was before. What's in the past is in the past, but at the same

time it was something I wanted to know about, and I did know most of it. I just wanted it confirmed. I like things nice and tidy – I don't like loose ends hanging around.

They feel they know their story now. However, there appear to be two ways of referring to this story: the first sees a life-history as comprising the one single narrative, about which they now have more detail and can fill in the gaps: the second is a life-history comprising two main threads of narrative, referring to the pre- and post-adoption selves. Those who talk in the first way, like the woman just quoted, are concerned more with their present lives and a search into the past enables them to deal with the present more easily, with more confidence. They want to find out whatever information is available and are happy to meet and incorporate their natural parents into their present lives, if possible. It is not something they regard themselves as *needing* to do however. As one woman said about applying for her birth certificate: 'Well, why not? It's available – just to see if there's anything else on there, like maybe a father's name.' Her purpose was simply to gain more information, to make her knowledge about herself, about her life-history, more complete. The same sense of completing the one story-line is evident in the words of another applicant: 'It was just curiosity, you know, where did I start out. It's odd really, but you know that's all it was.'

In contrast to this assimilation of knowledge from the past into current lives is the reaction of those adoptees who come to regard themselves as having two life-stories: that which they would have had with their real parents, under their real name, where they were really born; and that which they have had instead. Their interest appears to be in establishing the facts of the past in order to be able to calculate better their alternative life-history. 'I know the sort of life I did have, I know the sort of life I've got now – I wonder what sort of life I could have had.' The facts about their pre-adoption lives, which in many cases would cover only a matter of weeks, take a precedence over the events of their subsequent, post-adoption lives. The strength of this feeling is such that one 24-year-old man, adopted at the age of six weeks, argued, 'I had no idea of anything about myself.' It was as though their adoptive lives, however happy or unhappy, were seen as periods of living under a bogus identity: 'I would like to see what's going on. What the real story is.'

The word 'schizophrenic' was used by two adoptees in attempting to explain this feeling, but did not appear to convey distress felt, as much as the logic of their situation. It was for them a way of ordering lives which contained two of everything.

Although there are at least these two different ways of reacting to information about themselves, the adoptees share a newly acquired ability to recount their life-histories, whether this be done in terms of one single or two interwoven threads. Their social identity – that is, their ability to place themselves in their own and in the life-histories of others – becomes clearer. Section 26 is important in this process, not simply because it confers access to information but also because it allows for the public requesting of an account.

7 The Social Identity of Adoption

The meaning of access

The research upon which this book is based was undertaken to provide the knowledge inevitably missing from earlier discussions of Section 26: namely, who does the counselling, how is counselling done, how is counselling used by counsellors and counselled? In short, what patterns, if any, are emerging in the provision and use of Section 26? In addition, by studying in detail the providers' articulation of their practice and the users' reasons for their applications the *process* of counselling emerges. Awareness of the essentially dynamic nature of the interaction between counsellor and applicant leads to wider questions concerning the process of adoption in general. This chapter will examine the knowledge to be gained of adoption as a whole from a detailed study of this one particular aspect, access to birth records.

Section 26 counselling in effect translated the right to birth certificate information into a right to attempt to trace natural parents. An extension of this right to cover meeting natural parents was curtailed though. Questions of meeting became a case for individual persistence and negotiation between adoptee and natural parents (and sometimes the counsellor). What was seen in the parliamentary debate as an issue of children's rights versus parents' rights has beome, via counselling, an issue of moral responsibility, in terms of power and choice. The responsibility is shared by applicants, counsellors, natural parents and adoptive parents, but the bulk is shouldered by the adoptees:

> The curtains of confidentiality were to be officially drawn aside and the retrospective nature of the legislation, a matter of sharp controversy brought the concept of counselling and its limitations into focus. It was recognised that even at its best responsible counselling could not afford complete protection for the natural mother or father, if identity were traceable. Much, therefore, depended on the attitude of applicants with regard to tracing. (Day 1980: 28)

That counselling can benefit each of the parties concerned cannot be denied. Applicants feel their curiosity is vindicated as natural and approved of, at least by the counsellor; they feel, on the whole, that they are receiving professional and well-informed assistance in their enquiries, resulting not just in information but in support too. Adoptive and natural parents may derive reassurance from the existence of an intermediary body, which protects their privacy; they may even receive 'counselling' themselves on occasions. Counsellors benefit from the counselling by gaining knowledge of the adoptive experience which shows the results of past practice, which in turn informs current practice. Another effect of counselling is the setting of boundaries for responsible behaviour, which applicants and counsellors acknowledge even as they breach them – 'I overstepped the mark a bit' and 'I shouldn't have done that, really'. Some applicants slow down their enquiries in response to a counsellor's warnings; others decide to go on to trace having gained the public approval embodied in Section 26.

Such are the benefits of counselling, many of which were not foreseen by the parliamentarians and others who designed the legislation. They could act as *post hoc* justifications for linking compulsory counselling to access to birth records, but it is questionable whether they constitute adequate justification for obligatory counselling. The evidence of this study suggests that the original reasons for counselling – to ensure adoptees had adequately considered all the implications of making enquiries – were based on an unfounded fear: most applicants proved responsible.

The study also shows that Section 26 concerns more than access to birth records: it reveals crucial assumptions held about adopted people and adoption as a whole. In discussing the issues of access, practitioners, researchers and legislators make these assumptions explicit. In examining them more closely we learn not only more about the issue of access, but also more about the social place and role of adoption in our society.

'Natural' versus 'pathological' explanations for searching

Chapter 2 showed that research on access to birth records which informed the Houghton Committee and subsequent discussions presented a certain picture of adoptees which was accepted without much question. This implies that those who were so interested in their past as to wish actually to meet their natural parents were suffering in some way from a flawed, if not failed, adoption. Their wish was not the product of a natural curiosity but a 'deep psychological need' (Triseliotis 1973). Tracing and meeting were seen as some sort of self-therapy, correcting a psycho-pathological condition. However, this is not a picture to which our applicant interviewees conformed: our own assessment of them was as normal, well-adjusted adults; the counsellors' assessment of most of their counselling clients was 'surprisingly normal'; their own self-assessments fitted the 'naturally curious' category. We have seen their use of 'just-talk' to convey a rational approach, and even the one or two who described themselves as obsessed were not in any apparent sense pathologically so. Can we, therefore, posit an alternative explanatory framework to account for the actions of Section 26 applicants without resorting to the hitherto readily accepted reasoning? We believe there is such an explanation and one which will also explain the origins of the pathological model.

The rhetoric of the pathological model uses concepts such as the 'identity crisis' to describe the effect of a bad adoptive experience on the individual's ego identity, that private 'internal' sense of self. We argue that adoption can be better understood in terms of the individual's *social* identity: adoption is, after all, a social arrangement rather than a natural process happening to the individual. Strauss (1977) makes the point that identity, whatever it is, is concerned not simply with the internal workings of the mind, but with the external self also:

> Identity as a concept is fully elusive as is everyone's sense of his own personal identity. But whatever else it may be, identity is connected with the fateful appraisals made of oneself – by oneself and by others. Everyone presents himself to the others and to himself and sees himself in the mirrors of their judgements. (p. 9)

We suggest that restricting explanations to the concept of ego-identity is limited (and certainly fails to explain adequately the phenomenon we have studied). We turn instead to examine, in terms of adoption, 'how persons become implicated with other persons and are affected, and affect each other, through that implication' (Strauss 1977) People's social identity is precisely that which opens them to question, suspicion, friendliness, rejection, special-ness on the grounds of that which distinguishes them socially. For those with obvious distinguishing features the potential stress of interaction is far greater than for those who are apparently 'normal'. For the adopted person, unless they happen to possess some other highly visible signs of contextual abnormality, what distinguishes them from others is their adoptive status. We have seen in preceding chapters situations in which the fact of adoption has been socially damaging for some adoptees: on other occasions, adoption has been used to mark out an individual as special, someone who was specially chosen. Even this can separate someone out from the group as being different. We would suggest that enquiries that adoptees make about their past, including those under Section 26, signify an acknowledgement of their difference and further, present an attempt to account for it. In this way adopted people, though they cannot change their status of being different and in many cases would not want to, can at least repair any lacunae in their social identity arising from their failure to account for themselves. A social identity open to questioning does not imply, as a damaged ego identity might, a degree of psychological disturbance, but rather that extra care is required by the social act or interaction, and often that extra work is needed to ensure the individual is taken as a serious, competent but non-threatening member of society. It is precisely this sort of work that adoptees are performing in their 'just-talk'.

The adoption secret

The adoptive status of adoptees is of interest to others partly because the individual adoptee's social identity is inextricably caught up with the social identity of adoption as a whole. Just as the blind are associated with all sorts of special abilities, some spurious and some not, so there are many myths about adoption. However, our concern here is specifically with the social image of adoption and adoptees as held by practitioners, researchers and legislators. So we shall avoid lengthy consideration of the role of adoption in literature, and concentrate instead on the more prosaic but no less powerful identity of adoption as it arises through the legal and social structures in twentieth-century Britain. Chapter 2 has demonstrated that *de jure* adoption, that is, institutionally sanctioned adoption, has always been associated with the twin stigmata of infertility and illegitimacy. Consequently, it has also been associated with secrecy, which has served to preserve certain social standards of morality and normality, as well as, within certain constraints, the reputations of individuals. In the case of illegitimacy, social standards were preserved by separating, symbolically and physically, children from their past. Donzelot (1980) describes how this was accomplished in eighteenth-century France by the use of a special turret enabling unmarried mothers to abandon their children anonymously.

In this way the donor would not have been seen by any of the house staff. And this was the objective: to break, cleanly and without scandal, the original link identifying these individuals as the offspring of objectionable alliances, to cleanse social relations of progeny not in conformity with the law of the family, with its ambitions and its reputations. (p. 26)

In twentieth-century Britain the techniques are more subtle. The break occurs through the re-naming of the child, thereby immediately transforming what little social identity a baby has at that age and producing, through that same action, a fictionalised past biography. (This concept is borrowed and transformed from Glaser and Strauss (1965) who refer to the 'fictionalised future biography' created by the families of the terminally ill, who wish to disguise the status of dying from the patient. This situation has obvious parallels with the adoptive situation.) As Goffman (1963) argues, whenever a change in name occurs, 'an important breach is involved between the individual and his old world.' The breach was often physical, as well as metaphorical, as a baby could be placed in another county or country. Distant and distanced relatives indeed. Adoption then was arranged through different modes of institutionalised secrecy to disguise the fact of illegitimacy. As a consequence the fact of any infertility was also hidden. With the prescription to 'treat the child as if it were your own', adoptive parents were initially encouraged to keep the matter a secret within the family too. Their own feelings of failure and uncertainty arising from infertility provided encouragement to follow this advice.

Such were the circumstances under which many of our respondents were adopted in the 1940s and 1950s. Even when in the 1950s it was recognised that it was better to tell children they were adopted, on the basis that secrets within the family were not healthy and the knowledge that children tended to discover them anyway, the institutional secrecy remained in the form of changed names and secret registers. Adoptive parents were being given a double message: on the one hand they were told to be open with their children; on the other, they could witness that official secrecy persisted, and in some instances was increased. Adoptive parents were also, then as now, very dependent on the agencies for information about the natural parents. As there was a tendency in some cases to edit that information, including of course withholding the natural mother's name, adoptive parents did not always have the chance to be open with their children. Gaps in their knowledge resulted in gaps in the adoptees' knowledge. Historically, therefore, adoptees *and* adopters, through the linking of adoption with illegitimacy and infertility, were associated with stigma. The adopted child could, as a result, suffer on two levels: labelled illegitimate and thus suffer their natural parents' marginality, and labelled adopted, to suffer from their adopters' marginality. Any failing on the adoptive parents' behalf to be open with their child can be partly attributed to their awareness of their own and their child's potentially damaging social identity, and partly because of the double message they could witness institutionally. As Leeding (1980) says, 'The excessive secrecy of many adopters is a reflection of the adoption ethos of the past (p. 12). He feels this was particularly strong prior to the second world war, but we have seen it persisting through the 1940s and beyond.

The marginality of adoption

It might be argued that since the 1960s the social identity of adoption was such that the individual's identity need not suffer, since the stigma attached to illegitimacy and to infertility has diminished. However, the image of adoption, certainly to the audience about which we are writing, remains uncertain, as new worries replace old. Increasingly, concerns are expressed as to what is actually being done through the practice of adoption, and the separation of child from parent. Rautenan (1976) says of adoption, 'we have to face the fact that we establish relationships that are artificial . . . giving individuals new names and identities. We may really act as kinds of Gods . . .' (p. 27).

Such an interpretation is very difficult to face. Arguments continue about the relative importance of environment and heredity, the rights of natural parents versus adoptive parents, the paramount rights of the child, and even what is meant by parenting in the first place. As these arguments continue, no one can be totally confident about the social consequences of adoption. The questions are so profound that they are difficult to express, let alone answer, but the uneasiness is apparent in the difficulty experienced in placing or categorising different features of adoption. For example, the labels attached to the various parents are numerous: the birth parents, the natural parents, the original parents, the putative father; conversely, the adoptive parents, the social parents, the substitute parents.

The uneasiness about adoption *per se* attaches itself to the adoptees also, because of the fear that they might be damaged by the experience and also because they too are not easily placed in any one category. Since they are not rooted in natural relationships it is thought that there is no certainty about with whom they might align themselves: to natural or adoptive families, or perhaps to no one at all. They become sort of psychological vagrants, with no particular ties to anyone. The only feature by which they might be identified, and hence categorised, is their adoptive status – an adopted child – so they remain within that category.

> One of the common complaints of adopted adults is that they continued to be treated by society as 'children', they are never allowed to grow up. (Sorosky *et al.* 1978)

This spreads into all areas of the adoptee's life. Their calculations as to who their parents might be, or attempts to place themselves, come to be seen as fantasies; other attempts to discover information are regarded as potentially dangerous or even vindictive. Even when Section 26 empowered them to gain at least some information, they were still not regarded as sufficiently responsible and/or capable enough to cope with that sort of information, so special procedures involving age limits and counselling were established. The process of being adopted and of growing up adopted becomes then a process of being separated as a consequence of that status. Adoption is an experience of being different by virtue of membership of a statistic-ally-defined minority group; it is also the experience of being made marginal by a set of social processes embodied in the structural arrangements for adoption. For example, adopted children have their own, separate birth registers; adoption workers in social services departments are usually specialist workers, distinct from generic workers, often working in physically separate units or offices; adoption records are kept separately from other local authority records; adopted clients, especially under Section 26, are treated separately and differently from other local authority clients. Adop-tion, then, presents problems for practitioners and for society as a whole. Consequently adoptees also present a problem: we cannot place it or them easily. The uneasiness that is felt about the process is attributed to the individuals and extends to questioning their stability. In viewing adoptees potentially at least as damaged and in need of help, the psycho-pathological model attributes the

uncertainty about adoption to the adopted people themselves.
Conversely, the social identity model attributes the uncertainty to
the relationship between the adopted and the non-adopted:

> The attitudes we normals have towards a person with a stigma
> and the actions we take in regard to him, are well known, since
> these responses are what benevolent social action is designed to
> soften and ameliorate . . . we construct a stigma theory, an
> ideology to . . . account for the danger he represents. (Goffman
> 1963)

The ideology constructed for adoption is that of the individual
pathology of the identity crisis.

Adoptees' image of adoption

Just as adoptive parents have been aware of the image of adoption,
so have adopted people. Even as they use some of the same
language, such as searching for identity, they are eager to avoid the
worst aspects of the image: 'just-talk' removes the threat from their
actions. As Goffman points out,

> the stigmatised person learns and incorporates the standpoint of
> the normal, acquiring thereby the identity beliefs of the wider
> society and a general idea of what it would be like to possess a
> particular stigma. (Goffman 1963: 45)

We learn from a detailed study of Section 26 applicants that
though they are aware of the image and may even apply it to other
adoptees it is one they deny applies in general to themselves. They
have absorbed the norms of society to such an extent that they agree
with the necessity for compulsory counselling; but again, they as
individuals do not need it, though others might. In their own cases
they do not talk about themselves as trying to undo any damage
done to them by adoption, or even undo the adoption itself by
replacing their parents. Instead, to echo the applicant in Chapter 5,
'I'd like to see her to finish the story. . . . I like to know beginning,
middle and end, in general order.' Adoptees want a narrative in
order to place themselves in a continuum of their past, present and
future, which will account for and explain the possibilities of their
lives which underwent a shift, a disjuncture – even a displacement –
when they were placed for adoption. In most cases their adoption
relationships remain stable.

Tracers and non-tracers

The question arises, then, as to whether or not there is a difference between those adoptees who appear only to want information and those who want to trace natural parents. It has been suggested that the latter have suffered particularly badly in their adoptive relationships. However, as indicated earlier, we have seen that such a division is arbitrary and that many 'tracers' consider themselves to have had good, close relationships with their adopters. For the relationship between bad experience and tracing to hold the following factors should be demonstrated: first, there must be accurate predictions as to whether an adoptee will attempt to trace or not. We have seen that this is impossible since it is not an either/or situation for most adoptees, and factors such as time play an important part in deciding how far to go. Second, even if it were possible to divide adoptees in this way, relating intention to past experience would require a method of assessing that experience, in terms of its meaning for the individual, as opposed to its ability to measure up to an ideal of family life. Leeding (1980) has pointed out the difficulty of assessing adoptive as contrasted with normal family life. Third, how are the critical elements of that experience to be identified, and then assessed? Arguments range as to the relative importance of factors such as age at placement, age at telling, age of parents, number of siblings and so on. (For example, see Lawder (1969) and McWhinnie (1967).)

We have already seen that 'telling', for example, is far from straightforward even as a concept, let alone as a feature of interaction within actual families. Finally, the major weakness of the psycho-pathological argument is that it depends on a view of adoption that can be seen as having some sort of 'outcome' and a view of the adoptee who emerges from the adoptive family at the age of 18 with some form of fixed identity. It is almost as if once adoptees are adult, they are no longer affected by their adoptive relationships. It is very apparent from this study that adult adoptees consider their status and relationships to be very important throughout their lives, and that their reaction to it also develops throughout life as other circumstances change. The psycho-pathological argument is circular: a bad experience leads adoptees to trace, but the only 'proof' of that bad experience is the fact that the adoptee is tracing.

An alternative explanation is required to account for these actions: the concept of social identity helps to provide one. The wish for an account of one's life as an adopted person helps one to explain to self and others the circumstances of conception and birth. This results in an explanation of events that has placed the adoptee in a socially differentiated category. In order, however, to start making enquiries, even if only to ask adoptive parents for information, the adopted person must acknowledge (to self as to others by virtue of the questions) this feature of social identity. It is, in Kirk's (1964) term, an 'acknowledgement-of-difference'. Having recognised the fact, there appears to be little distinction between the desire to acquire information and the desire to trace. What is different is what counts for adoptees as the source and constituents of an adequate account. For some, the official records have a stability and certainty which stories given by members of their families lack. For others, official information has been so patchy and grudgingly given that the only reliable source is seen to be the natural mother herself. What is important in MacIntyre's version of the 'narratable self' is that through the acknowledgement of difference, adoptees are able to begin to ask others for an account and to incorporate that account in their hitherto patchy life-history (MacIntyre 1981).

It is not, therefore, points along a continuum of need that mark off whether a person will trace or not. It is other social factors that might cause them to desist from tracing, or even to desist from making any enquiries at all. An 'enquirer but non-tracer' might resist tracing not just out of a desire not to hurt the adopters, but also because of the nature of that hurt. Enquiries force adopters, as much as adoptees, to confront their own social identity of 'difference', and this can be painful. Also the risk of being thought odd or obsessive is enough to hold back other enquirers, as well, of course, as the fear of disrupting natural parents' lives and of being rejected.

What then of the non-enquirers: why are they apparently 'not interested' (Triseliotis 1984) in their natural parents? First of all, the question is whether or not there is such a person as a non-enquirer. There are certainly many adoptees who do not make official Section 26 enquiries, but very few who, once they know they are adopted, do not ask what that means. For those who do not make official enquiries one can posit the same arguments as to what holds them back as those which distinguish the enquirers from the tracers. Additional factors would perhaps include a dislike of bureaucracy (Walby 1982), a dislike of social workers, and a dislike of becoming a social work 'client'. However, those adopters who do not make any enquiries at all as they reach adolescence and adulthood are perhaps far from the emotionally mature and stable adults that the logical extension of the pathology model would suggest. They might in fact be refusing to acknowledge their difference, preferring instead Kirk's idea of a 'rejection-of-difference'. Perhaps we should be examining more closely why adopted people do not trace rather than seeing those that do as an aberration of the process.

The key factor, then, in the social identity of adoption is its differentness: as Stone (1969) argues, there is nothing pathogenic in adoption *per se*. Adoptees have much in common with other social groups or affiliations that experience difference, and in some contexts marginality. The blind and the terminally ill have already been mentioned. Much can be learnt about adoption by comparing the societal reactions to these people and by comparing the strategies with which they cope with those reactions, and the problems that remain. In discussing the 'management of spoiled identity', Goffman (1963) describes just one of many problems that adoptive parents and adoption workers share with these other groups.

> Parents, knowing of their child's stigmatic condition may encapsulate him with domestic acceptance and ignorance of what he is going to have to become. When he ventures outdoors he does so therefore as an unwitting passer, at least to the extent that his stigma is not immediately apparent. At this point his parents are faced with a basic dilemma regarding information management, sometimes appealing to medical practitioners for strategies. If the child is informed about himself at school age, it is felt that he may not be strong enough psychologically to bear the news, and in addition may tactlessly disclose these facts about himself to those who need not know. On the other hand, if he is kept too long in the dark, then he will not be prepared for what is to happen to him and moreover may be informed about his condition by strangers who have no reason to take the time and care required to present the facts in a constructive, hopeful light. (p. 113)

Those who feel that the language of stigma is too strong to be applied to adoption should note that other groups cited by Goffman include those who are physically-handicapped, Jewish, black, white, male or female: in other words, the stigma lies not within the characteristics of the group but in the characteristics of the social context in which a member of a particular social category is identified as being different from the majority. Some individuals will experience this more frequently than others, but each individual's social identity is potentially at risk.

The important point to add about adoption is that the social organisation of adoption and the assumptions of adoption practitioners and researchers actually help to create additional situations for the adoptee to negotiate, in order to display their mental stability and thus prove their competence to handle apparently 'dangerous' information.

Implications for practice

It is clear from what has been written so far that practitioners and researchers need a wider concept of adoption to take into account issues of social identity, rather than use a restricted psychological model. We should reconsider and accept (or change) what it is that adoption actually is, rather than skirt around that and assume that better practice will result in better adoptions. As Jane Rowe (undated) has said, 'there has been less discussion on what adoption really is than on whether or not it has been successful.' It is not surprising that the balance of concern would be tipped this way, however, as those involved want to know whether or not it 'works'. Acknowledging that problems sometimes do arise and placements do fail only encourages them to work harder at improving the techniques involved. The alternative would be to ask if we should even have adoption. Given some of the alternatives, such as residential care or a succession of foster homes, this would perhaps be too unnerving a question to expect practitioners to ask, let alone answer. It is rather a question for policy-makers and will be considered in the next chapter: here our concern is with practitioners, though their experiences should inform legislation.

Much research has been conducted into adoption and a large part of it has assessed one or other aspect thought to affect outcome. Overwhelmingly the answer has been that, yes, it does work overall, and to point out areas that could improve 'satisfaction' with adoption or even to improve the 'adoptability' of certain children. Besides sounding slightly as if a commodity was being discussed (although this is not that far removed from how some adoptees, without rancour, view their function in their parents' lives), the general tone of the literature is one of reassurance. This is particularly strong in discussions of access, where much of the reassurance is directed to adoptive parents and practitioners. For example, Triseliotis (1984) says,

Neither should the wish for access to birth records be seen as reflecting on the parenting qualities of the adoptive family. The figures, after all, suggest that the wish for access remains a minority response among adoptees and those hoping for reunions with the original parent(s) are still fewer. Available evidence also suggests that the results of reunions are mixed, i.e. that many contacts are broken off soon after they are established. (pp. 6–7)

The argument here and elsewhere is that since so few apply, and those that do have suffered a flawed adoption, the majority of adoptions must be 'all right'. This may be reassuring (if perhaps inaccurate?) to social workers and adoptive parents, but it is quite the opposite to adoptees who have already experienced other pressures not to pursue what they regard as a 'natural curiosity'.

Because there are apparently so few alternatives to adoption the literature of reassurance strays also into a literature of advocacy, representing an idealised case. For example, Rowe argues,

An adoption cannot be legalised until the natural parents have agreed to lay down their rights and responsibilities. Thus the adopted child truly has only one set of parents though others gave him life. (p.95)

Stating the legal case unfortunately does not remove all other meanings that individuals will attach to certain situations and certain people. Similarly, Triseliotis (1984) says, 'the people who matter to adoptees are those who bring them up and not those who gave birth to them.' Although 'matter' in this context is a loaded word, natural parents play a very important role in the adoptee's life, even in their absence, so to deny this is perhaps to convey a misunderstanding of adoption.

This view of adoption is based on the assumption that there is such a condition as 'outcome' and that its nature is dependent on intra-familial interaction, rather than any wider social factors. The result is that more emphasis is laid on working with adoptive parents, such as trying to ensure that they can accept the child's background, that they can provide adequate parenting: important of course, but still restricted to an intra-familial notion of development. This can also lead to the temptation of assuming all is well within present practice because of these improvements. What needs to be added to this picture is an awareness by practitioners of the effect of their own practices, structures and assumptions. Perhaps if it is accepted that adoptees, for example, who apply under Section 26 are not 'suffering' in some way, questions such as how much information to release and of what type are more easily resolved. Equally, it might also be recognised that questions such as these are tied up as much with the identity and uncertainties of social work, as with a wish to protect their clients, both visible and invisible. Rautenan (1976) argues,

> I think they are entitled to know all about their background. The situation may be difficult for the social workers. Perhaps it is due to our training that we would want to protect our client from the knowledge of real rejection, abandonment, social squalor and disease, particularly mental disease. However, in this kind of work, it is not possible and we may not even be able to stop the client from coming into direct contact with such circumstances. Also we have learned through experience that it is no use trying to make things 'nicer' for everyone. The only thing we can do is to try to understand reality and interpret this understanding to the client. (pp. 23–4)

The pressures on the social workers when considering what information to release are very similar to those on adoptive parents in 'telling' and also of adoptees in telling adopters about their enquiries. Each reflects the uncertainty about the meaning of adoption and about their own social identity. For social workers the task is to decide not only what is best for the client but also what is best in terms of upholding certain standards of professional judgement and responsibility. One counsellor argued that confidentiality was simply a prop or a screen for practitioners to hide behind. Adoption is one area of work where these decisions are flung into sharp relief, being a piece of work that is both attractive and also 'dangerous'. Evidence of the multiple and overlapping categories that come into play is given by the uncertainty of labelling applicants as 'clients'. It should be recognised, however, that those adoptees who are most worrying in counselling are in fact worrying for features other than their adoptive status: they are adolescents, or aggressive or mentally unstable. It is examples such as these that should lead to questioning of assumptions about adoption and to new explanatory frameworks. Above all, practitioners should be aware of making the mistake they charge adoptive parents with making: that is, assuming that because adoptive applicants do not come to them with their enquiries that they are simply not interested. The complexity of adoption requires a more subtle approach.

Practitioners and researchers therefore may gain more from operating with a psycho-social model of identity, to understand adoption as a whole and the question of tracing in particular. However, practitioners work within a context of certain legislation and social policies. In our final chapter we turn to a discussion of what can be learnt about the policies on adoption using a social identity model, and what this can tell us not only about the present and future policies in adoption but in child care in general.

8 Social and Biological Families: Implications for Policy

Introduction

Chapter 7 showed that to experience adoption is also to experience difference: an adopted person has been reared by social rather than biological parents, and this has been accentuated by the surrounding secrecy. The experience of being *made* different also affects adoptive and natural parents. Increasingly, however, other people are experiencing a similar situation, through divorce and re-marriage and also through state intervention in forms of public child care. Moreover, developments in adoption since the mid-1970s are such that the distinction between adoption and other forms of child care are becoming blurred, and as the choices of forms of care broaden, the boundaries between natural and social parenting also blur and overlap.

The use of Section 26 can be seen as the expression of a wish, both institutional and individual, to deal with the complexities of relationships in families where social and biological parenting are experienced. As such it can indicate some of the possible current and future experiences of children brought up in families like this. This chapter will explore those possibilities and examine their implications for future child care practice. We shall look at three general areas: first, adoption itself because it is in a period of flux which make it critical to explore the likely experiences of future adoptees and see what this means for the use of legislation like Section 26; second, other forms of child care such as long-term fostering, to see to what extent they overlap with adoption; finally, we shall look at artificial insemination by donor and *in vitro* fertilisation. Though these last two are not forms of child care as such, they are seen as a solution to infertility and are a key type of social/biological parenting. Consequently, comparisons have been made with adoption and these will be explored.

Adoption

Section 26 exposes the artifice of adoption not only to the family members, but also institutionally. In Kirk's (1964) words, it represents an institutional 'acknowledgement-of-difference' in a way that the changing of names and the secrecy involved refuses to do. As a piece of legislation it also highlights the contradiction between policy and practice, in which individual adoptees and adoptive parents are involved; they are enjoined to be open and honest within the family, whilst institutionally secrecy is advocated and maintained.

Recent developments in adoption practice accentuate this contradiction since they make the fact of adoption more visible socially. For example, advances in the notion of 'adoptability' have meant that a greater number of formerly 'hard-to-place' children who had, in a sense, no place in society, are being found homes. The emphasis in practice is now clearly on homes for children rather than children for an infertile couple. Consequently, different criteria exist for placements, such that they do not necessarily reproduce the patterns (temporal, physical, genetic) of normal family life that earlier adoptions at least attempted. For example, children would often be placed in descending age-order and with such gaps between their ages that they could physically have been borne by the same woman. Such steps were taken even after 'matching' for physical likenesses was supposed to be a thing of the past. Now older children are beginning to dominate the adoption figures: in 1981, 50 per cent of adoptions were of children aged 5–14 years. Equally, mixed-race or ethnic minority children, groups of siblings, and physically and mentally handicapped children are being found adoptive homes far more easily than was first imagined possible (OPCS 1983). This, of course, affects the nature of those adoptions, the sheer visibility of the adoptive family bringing to an end, to some extent at least, the secrecy which was tempting for traditional adopters.

The nature of adoptive parenting has also changed, so that the demands made of parents are very different and quite possibly far more difficult. Hence the range of choice of adopters has broadened so that, for example, some older couples who appear particularly suitable for a certain child will be accepted, whereas before they might have been turned away simply because of their age. The notion of the 'professional parent' is now used in some local authorities to denote the different criteria for selection and also to fit in with the new schemes available for the payment of adopters in some circumstances. Increasingly the notion of 'open' or 'inclusive' adoptions is canvassed where natural parents retain contact with their child after the child has been adopted.

Concepts such as 'parenting' and 'families' are becoming much more diffuse as practices such as these continue and increase. The responsibilities, rights and duties of the individuals in these circumstances change accordingly. These developments have not occurred without comment from non-practitioners. For example, weekly payments to adopters (as in fostering) for some categories of children has had a mixed reaction, particularly from those who fear the intrusion of commercial criteria into family life and into adoption in particular, since it is perceived as undermining one of the basic principles. Being paid to look after other people's children is common, either as a salary or an allowance against expenses, such as in child-minding or fostering: being paid to look after one's own children is thought to go against the basic reasons for having those children in the first place.

These developments are important for the consideration of adoption in the future. Will they, for example, affect the future use of Section 26? On the basis of the optimism expressed by many practitioners during the course of this study it could be argued that present practice of telling adoptees about their status is now so good that there will be little need for Section 26 and certainly for counselling in the future. This is based, however, on the idea that most people just want information of the sort their adoptive parents are given by practitioners at time of placement, assuming that is, that the information has been passed on. We have seen that the usage of the law is more complex than this, though it is likely that without compulsory counselling the formal enquiries will play even less of a part of the total search than they do now. For many enquiries are likely to provide confirmation rather than discovery, though the process of adoption will still be something that affects their personal and social identity. Also those adopted at an older age will still need to know the reasons behind their placement up to that point. It is difficult to calculate even now the numbers of Section 26 applicants as a percentage of the total, so the future take-up rate is even more difficult to predict, though the take-up rate for *voluntary* counselling is likely to be less than the total of those actually applying under Section 26. In some current calculations the number of step-parent adoptions has sometimes been left out of the calculations on the basis that they do not need to apply. However, we have seen that even those adoptees who know all the facts about their background, including some step-parent adoptees, still applied under Section 26 because of the meaning the law has for them. Therefore, in future calculations, where similar judgements might be made about, for example, inclusive adoptions, there will be a need to re-examine the reasons for usage from the applicants' perspectives. There is little reason to suppose either that a rush of 18-year-olds will occur since the constraints against them doing so, namely a wish to protect adoptive parents particularly whilst still living in the same home, are as likely to exist then as now. However open parents have been in the past, adoptees have still been reluctant to do anything to hurt them.

In terms of adoption practice in general, there is a risk with these developments that two styles of adoption will develop: that for the placing of young babies and that for the placing of the older child, especially with the continuance of institutional secrecy over the birth certificate. Whilst older children will remember their previous name and will, therefore, require explanations for the change, the baby will undergo the change unknowingly and will remain dependent on the adoptive parents for any information. For any adult enquiring under Section 26 in the future (and if placed after November 1975) routes to detailed information will be more difficult without a counsellor as a guide. Conversely, the difficulties for the social worker holding the adoption files will begin when the adoptee has found the route, for then the judgement of how much information to give, difficult enough now, will be crucial. For some a precedent will have been set at the time of placement and the information given to adoptive parents then, but the problem becomes more acute when the adult adoptee is sitting across the desk. Up to now the nature of the difficulty has been to tell someone they were illegitimate. Some of the handling of this was eased, if rather crudely, by the absence of the father's name on the birth certificate. However, many adoptees had already worked this out and for others it was not very important anyway, given their other interests and perhaps the social climate. Does this mean though that children currently being placed will be able to work out along similar lines that they had perhaps been neglected or physically abused by their natural parent(s)? Or that they had been the subject of a contested adoption? Social workers will have to confront those facts themselves first and decide how much and in what way they will be able to tell a person face-to-face. There is a temptation to withhold information in order to protect the client, but how much is this a need to protect themselves first? These issues are currently very important as the campaign for easier access to local authority files gains ground. Perhaps different counselling strategies will emerge to cope with these problems.

It is quite likely that the voluntary adoption agencies which have gained the right to do Section 26 counselling (from 1982) will develop their own counselling strategies in the light of the type of information they hold. Negotiations between local authorities and voluntary agencies need to be more carefully worked out in the future than they have been so far, given the claims to 'ownership' each puts on the applicant and on the records. Rules of confidentiality should be assessed to see whose needs they best serve.

Practitioners will also need to confirm or otherwise their satisfaction with legislation such as Section 26, since they could be very influential in deciding the future of openness in adoption. For example, the suggestion has been mooted in various quarters, not least by John Stroud (1983), that the legislation should be extended in some ways, at least to siblings of adoptees, if not to natural parents themselves. Issues such as these are important for their own sake and also because they need to be considered as part of the development of all local authority adoption services, as required by Section 1 of the Children Act. For example, practitioners should consider the suggestion that they should continue to be in contact with adoptive families after the order has been finalised. This, too, breaks with the traditional idea that the adoptive family should be just like any other and not have social work contact just because of its adoptive status. The other suggestions to be considered for future adoption services from the Children Act, though not yet implemented, are those concerning custodianship as an alternative to adoption.

In brief, the traditional assumptions and concepts of adoption are gradually being eroded to be replaced with new ideas aimed at protecting the best interests of the child. This has changed adoption radically and brought concepts such as family, parenting and even child care itself under critical consideration. It has also raised questions as to the rights of the other parties involved, mostly those of the natural parents. This is an issue of particular concern to child care in general and in the process of finding some answers we again return to the issues of natural versus social parenting.

Other forms of child care

In the course of the research project counsellors reported an increase in the numbers of enquiries about their backgrounds from children who were currently in residential care and from adults who had been in care. They had been aware of the publicity given to Section 26 and obviously felt it could apply to them. As our research demonstrates adoptees feel conflict over the relative importance of natural and adoptive parents, and their place in each family. Such a conflict must apply to the residential care child or foster child. Indeed the problems could be even more acute in the latter cases because they will tend to experience multiple rather than double parenting. Indeed, for those in residential care these 'parents' will very often only be staff on shifts and their 'siblings' children from other families in the same position as themselves. Those children and those who experience short-term foster care placements are liable to suffer more psychological damage than that purported to arise from adoption owing to a sense of a 'precarious self', heightened by movements between families. The need for a narrative sense of self, so important in adoption, is more so in these situations, in order to place all these changes and make sense of them in a comprehensive and comprehensible life-history. This partly accounts for the success of life-story books for children and their increased use can only be encouraged, but the question remains as to what to put in them and when.

However, despite these needs, and the partial recognition of them at least at the level of practice, there is no legislative provision to satisfy them, or even any systematic practice. This is partly to do with the status of these forms of care, particularly residential care, which is not as attractive as adoption, either in the public imagination or even for practitioners. Children in care also suffer from the stigma that their circumstances are in many ways taken to reflect on them, rather than on the actions of the adults in their lives. The failure to provide solutions to their situation might stem also from the assumption that residential care is only a short-term provision in most cases and that for other cases there is no alternative. Rowe's (1973) research has shown clearly that this is not so: children who remained in care for longer than six months had only a 25 per cent chance of being returned to their natural parents.

The previous section has indicated the impact this study had on child care and adoption, leading to an ever-widening scope for these measures. Seed (1981) shows the choices now available in child care and they include adoption, fostering with a view to adoption, long-term fostering, short-term fostering and residential care. Each of these has an additional dimension, as to whether they will be inclusive or exclusive with regard to natural parent contact. Each of these alternatives, especially in current practice, reflects a shift in emphasis, certainly since 1975, from attempting to rehabilitate the child with the natural parents towards placing that child in a situation of permanent social parenting. This change was reflected in other areas of the 1975 Act, such as the removal of natural parents' rights to place their child for a private adoption; the assumption of parental rights by local authorities; the freeing of a child for adoption; and finally the payment of allowances to adoptive parents to make all these other moves easier in practice and in consequence.

The importance of these measures cannot be over-emphasised since they are potentially applicable to all natural parents. They also represent major changes for social workers, many of whom have a great sympathy for the difficulties of natural parents. This can and has led to conflict within the same authority between those workers involved with the natural families and those involved in making placements for adoption. Whilst the former hope for rehabilitation the latter argue for the benefits of a permanent caring relationship. Like Section 26 these difficulties can become an issue of the rights of the natural parents versus the rights of their children. And, as with Section 26, a further dimension of confusion is added by a consideration of the rights of the foster parents (in Section 26, the rights of the adoptive parents). The conflict aroused in some practitioners, especially by the finality of adoption, has been immense and practice has varied widely (Rowe 1976). This has led to much public (*Guardian* 1982) and professional concern. There are also constraints on the professionals which sometimes hinder their practice. Besides the organisational difficulties there are conflicts between what the individual social worker feels is right, what current practice demands and what administration allows, given limited resources. Then there are legislative constraints and demands. Does the knowledge that certain powers accrue to the local authority over time, within each individual child's career in care, affect the short- and long-term planning that might take place for that child? Does legislation follow on from practice, or does it dictate practice?

Decisions about child care also take place within the wider societal context and developments in that context impinge on social work decisions. It is relevant, therefore, to consider the fact that one in eight families is now headed by a single parent and that 60 per cent of divorces involve dependent children, so 'a significant minority of children can expect to experience separation from one or other of their natural parents and in some cases from their brothers and sisters' (Rimmer 1981). Even though social workers may not be directly involved in these situations the knowledge that they exist and that they come about without social work intervention must impinge on their decisions. Similarly, developments within the medical construction of families, such as artificial insemination by donor and *in vitro* fertilisation, highlight for social work practitioners the way other professionals treat the issues of social versus natural parenting. This can only help to clarify the dilemmas they feel and perhaps provide some solutions.

Artificial insemination by donor/*in vitro* fertilisation

In considering AID as a comparison with adoption it is important to remember that it is not primarily a form of child care, in as much as it is not designed to serve the needs of an existing child. It is, instead, a solution to the needs of couples who are unable to have their own children. Thus it overlaps with one side of traditional adoption, but the side which is becoming less important. Because of the developments within adoption, however, AID becomes a course more seriously considered for the couple who are unable to adopt. On the other hand, there are certain similarities between the two in as much as once the process has been completed, the tension of natural and social parenting exists and debates as to whether or not such children should be told about their origins often translate into the issue of children's versus parents' needs. It is, then, an area relevant to family policy, if not directly to child care.

In AID the husband/partner of the woman being inseminated is not the genetic father of the resultant child, whereas the woman is the genetic mother. However, institutionally, that fact is usually disguised by 'allowing' the husband to be named as father on the birth certificate, even though this is in fact breaking the law. The donor is also allowed to remain anonymous. The grounds for this are both psychological and practical. There is a wish to avoid exposing the man as infertile; to avoid stigmatising the child by the label 'an AID child'; there is a fear that the donor system would collapse if donors knew they were to be identified. The similarities to the debates in adoption are clear: a build-up of social secrecy because of the fear of stigma and a fear that the source of adopters would diminish if adoption were made open. These arguments were raised even as recently as the parliamentary debates on the 1975 Children Act. We have seen, however, that in adoption at least the aura of secrecy serves only to increase the stigma through a sense of fear and shame.

The donor, however, is very much the unknown quantity in this procedure. Most of the debates about the morality of AID concern the husband and the child, particularly the latter. The donor though is in a very ambiguous position of being both public benefactor but also socially suspect given the procedures involved in fulfilling his role. Indeed, the Feversham Commitee (1960) argued, 'We feel that the role of donor is of such a kind that it is liable to appeal to the abnormal and the unbalanced.' Certainly, those doctors who call for the retention of anonymity argue that those donors who do not mind being identified are psychologically suspect. There are also legal implications for identifying the donor, given the possibility of the mother and child seeking affiliation orders for financial support. This problem is easily resolved, however, by the adoption by the mother's partner of the child after birth.

This course of action would also solve one of the fears expressed on the child's behalf, that the child would be illegitimate as a result of AID. Whether or not this is still a problem is debatable, given the example of adoption. What is more likely to cause problems is the suspicion aroused within the family by the parental collusion. As Pincus and Dare (1978) argue,

> Secrets and myths may . . . be started by an individual member of the family. Like everything else that happens in families, they do not remain the property of the individual, as the responses of other family members set in motion processes of interaction, which strengthen or weaken the effects of secrets and myths. (p. 16)

Children or adults are likely to suspect something, not just through family interaction but also through basic genetic knowledge. Other temporal and social, as well as physical cues work to confirm their suspicion, but given the lack of publicity of AID until recently, they are far more likely to suspect adoption or even adultery, rather than the truth.

Although the child is the acceptable cause for concern, it is rather more likely that the woman's partner and the practitioners are the ones who seek protection through secrecy. It is argued that whilst it is acceptable for a woman to be identified as infertile, it is not so for a man given some confusion between infertility and impotence. Not only would openness thus stigmatise the man, it would also ruin his relationship with the child. There was little evidence that the adoptees we spoke to felt any contempt or similar feelings about their adoptive parents, simply because they were unable to have their own children. However, members of a national organisation for the childless, who are likely to be key users of the AID provisions, were overwhelmingly in favour of secrecy (Owens 1982–3).

Practitioners are also in favour of secrecy of AID, over and beyond the level of confidentiality traditionally expected from medical practitioners. There is some unease about the procedure, and many practitioners have rigorous criteria for the selection of couples thought suitable (Snowden and Mitchell 1981). The selection of donors, however, appears to be far less rigorous. The justification for AID is that it solves a problem of sub-fertility or of genetic disorders, but it is not a system they are otherwise generally very happy about. A lack of publicity, coupled with highly confidential records plus the anonymity of the donor represents this uneasiness. It has been argued (Joyce 1982) that were AID to become 'open', practitioners would not cooperate and would even destroy the records they possessed. The status of the medical profession is such that doctors are able to keep tight control over the confidentiality of their records, which social workers are unable to do, even if they should wish.

Whether the children have a right to know their genetic origins, possibly at the expense of the adults involved, is a debate that was thoroughly rehearsed prior to the introduction of Section 26. It would seem that Section 26 is the answer. It is difficult to argue a special case for AID. Looking at Section 26, however, should also provide reassurance for the AID couple, practitioner and donor. This is not the false reassurance along the lines of 'so few people apply . . . ' but reassurance which comes through explanation and hence understanding. That is, that the enquiries represent a desire on the enquirers' part to place themselves socially, not to replace the parents.

A brief note should also be added on the process of *in vitro* fertilisation where currently most cases involve the couple as genetic parents, using a procedure which simply aids the fertilisation process. However, logically, any egg and any sperm can be fertilised and placed inside any woman. Thus the categories of parenting become even more confused. Snowden and Mitchell (1981) point out that the five stages of producing a child – those of female and male genitor, female carrier, mother and father – can now logically be carried out by five different people.

The implications for social work practitioners of AID/IVF are less in terms of what they can do, as in what they can learn from possible extreme examples of the mixing of social and biological parenting, for their own practice in adoption and fostering. They can also teach AID workers from that experience. Some AID clinics now have social workers attached as counsellors and their practice needs to be examined. What would be the implications of one section of a profession advocating openness whilst another section advocates secrecy? As a professional body, as well as groupings of practitioners, social work would benefit from an appraisal of current practice in this field.

Conclusion

By mixing biological and social parenting in families we are creating ambiguous relationships, the nature of which those who are affected need to know. Adopted people are concerned with defining who counts as their 'real' mother and the interesting point, for adoption and also for all these other forms of care just discussed, is not whom they decide upon (some will say the adoptive mother, others the natural mother) but that they have to ask the question in the first place. In other words concepts such as mother, father and family do not possess any form of absolute meaning but are problematic. It is only when the contrast between natural and social emerges that we can see this clearly. In the case of adoption and Section 26 the child had no choice about the transfer from one set of parents to another: the fear which surrounded Section 26 was that the adult adoptee did now have that power to choose. For the adoptee, however, curiosity stems less from a wish to choose as from a wish to understand. The problem for the adopted person is that, in seeking to understand, the nature of the dilemma has to be accepted in the first place. For some it is easier not to. For those who do go so far as to confront the dilemma, some will call their natural parents by their first names, and reserve the titles 'Mum and Dad' for their social parents.

The adoptee has to confront and resolve issues which gain little public acknowledgement. Secrecy serves to protect all those involved, family and professionals, but can lead to its own problems: that of maintaining the secrecy on all levels and that of coping with the breakdown of secrecy, either intentional or unintentional. There would be little need for Sections 26 if birth certificates had not been changed and kept secret in the first place. Instead of automatically advocating confidentiality (itself a particular form of secrecy) the questions to ask are what is it for, and who benefits/suffers from it? The argument that the child must be protected has two weaknesses: the first is that illegitimacy and similar stigmata arise only out of the actions of the adults, not of the child. Once society stops using the circumstances of the child's conception as a reflection of personal qualities there will be little stigma from adoption, fostering or AID. The moves by the Law Society to remove the label of illegitimacy are a welcome first step. The second weakness is that far from being protected socially by their adoptive parents, it is the child who frequently protects the parents, intentionally by avoiding certain topics of conversation and by not telling the parents about adoption enquiries, and also unintentionally by being the subject of provisions such as counselling, where the parents are the invisible clients. The problem of secrecy in general is that it promotes further secrecy.

Parents also suffer in these proceedings, particularly natural parents, and it has been argued, by one of our adoptee interviewees amongst others, that child care is effectively the relocating of children from the socially non-sanctioned to the sanctioned. Certainly, the rights of natural parents, generally as well as in the field of child care, have been progressively curtailed through state intervention. Whether morally right or wrong, it is the fact that, for example, one cannot change one's name at will or give up one's child at will: the state through the public construction of families can do both.

What we have seen in this study and in its application to other areas of child care is that 'the family' as a single concept fails to account for the complex relationships that can be created socially. We follow Donzelot (1980) when he argues that the family should be seen,

> not as a point of departure, as a manifest reality, but as a moving resultant, an uncertain form whose intelligibility can only come from studying the system of relations it maintains with the sociopolitical level. This requires us to detect all the political mediations that exist between the two registers, to identify the lines of transformation that are situated in that space of intersections.
>
> Following these lines of transformation we see the contours of a form of sociality gradually taking shape, one that will furnish a tangible surface, an effective plane for understanding the present-day family, its variations, its fragility and its strength, its incentives and its inertia. We thereby gain a clearer idea of the destiny of the family form in liberal societies. (p. xxv)

Bibliography

ABAA (1971) 'Comments of members on the working paper "Adoption of Children" ' (Association of British Adoption Agencies, March).

ABAA (1975a) 'Notes and comments on the Children Bill' (Association of British Adoption Agencies).

ABAA (1975b) 'Further comments on the Children Bill' (Association of British Adoption Agencies).

ABAFA (1976) 'The search for identity: the adopted person's need for information about his origins' (Association of British Adoption and Fostering Agencies, August).

ABAFA (n.d.) 'Child adoption: a selection of articles on adoption theory and practice' (Association of British Adoption and Fostering Agencies).

ADSS (1975) 'Comment on the Children Bill' (Association of Directors of Social Services).

Abrams, P. (1977) 'Community care: some research problems and priorities', in Barnes, J. and Connolly, N. (eds), *Social Care Research* (Bedford Square Press).

Adcock, M., White, R. and Rowlands, O. (1982) *The Administrative Parent. A study of the assumption of parental rights and duties* (British Agencies for Adoption and Fostering, June).

Aumend, S. A. and Barrett, M. C. (1983) 'Searching and non-searching adoptees', in *Adoption and Fostering*, vol. 7, no. 2.

BASW (1975) 'Analysis of the Children Bill' (British Association of Social Workers).

Barclay Report, The (1982) *Social Workers: their role and tasks* (Bedford Square Press).

Benet, M. K. (1976) *The Politics of Adoption* (Free Press).

Berger, M. and Hodges, J. (1982) 'Some thoughts on the question of when to tell the child that he is adopted', in *Journal of Child Psychotherapy*, vol. 8.

Bevan, H. K. and Parry, M. L. (1978) *Children Act, 1975* (Butterworths).

Brandon, J. and Warner, J. (1977) 'AID and adoption: some comparisons', in *British Journal of Social Work*, vol. 7, no. 3.

Day, C. (1980) 'General Register Office study', in Hall, T. (ed.), *Access to Birth Records* (Association of British Adoption and Fostering Agencies).

DHSS (1976) 'Children Act 1975: implementation of Section 26, access by adopted people to birth records' (LAC(76)21, Department of Health and Social Security).

Dixon, Samuel L. and Sands, Robert G. (1983) 'Identity and the experience of crisis', in *Social Casework*, vol. 64, no. 4 (April).

Donzelot, J. (1980) *The Policing of Families: welfare versus the state* (Hutchinson).

Edgar, M. (1976) 'Black child and white family', in *The Search for Identity* (Association of British Adoption Agencies).

Eekelaar, J. (1983) 'Parents and children: rights, responsibilities and needs', in *Adoption and Fostering*, vol. 7, no. 2.

Ehrlich, H. (1977) *A Time to Search* (Paddington Press).

Feversham Committee (1960) 'Report of the Departmental Committee on human artificial insemination', Cmnd 1105 (HMSO).

Fisher, F. (1973) *In Search of Anna Fisher* (New York: Arthur Fields).

Foucault, M. (1976) *The History of Sexuality, vol. 1: An Introduction* (Pelican edn, 1981).

Gaskins, R. (1981) 'The role of discretion in the legal and social service systems', in *Social Casework: The Journal of Contemporary Social Work* (September).

Goffman, E. (1963) *Stigma: Notes on the management of spoiled identity* (Prentice Hall).

Greenwood, E. (1966) 'Attributes of a profession', in Vollmer, H. N. and Mills, D. L. (eds), *Professionalisation* (Prentice Hall).

Guardian, The (1982) 'Crisis in child care' (3, 10 and 17 November).

Haimes, E. V. and Timms, N. W. (1983) 'Access to birth records and counselling of adopted persons under Section 26 of the Children Act, 1975' (Final Report to the Department of Health and Social Security, May).

Hall, T. (ed.) (1980) 'Access to birth records: the impact of Section 26 of the Children Act, 1975' (Association of British Adoption and Fostering Agencies, Research Series 1).

Halmos, P. (1965) *The Faith of the Counsellors* (Constable).

Hardy, B. (1968) 'Towards a poetic of fiction: An approach through narrative', in *Novel*, 2, 5–14.

HMSO (1976) *Access to Birth Records. Notes for Counsellors.*

HMSO (1976) *Access to Birth Records. Information for Adopted People.*

Houghton Committee (1970) 'Adoption of children: working paper of the Departmental Committee on the Adoption of Children' (HMSO).

Houghton Report (1972) 'Report of the Departmental Committee on the Adoption of Children', Cmnd 5107 (HMSO, October).

Hurst Report (1954) 'Report of the Departmental Committee on the adoption of children' (HMSO).

Jacka, A. A. (1973) *Adoption in Brief: an annotated bibliography, 1966–72* (National Children's Bureau, NFER).

Joyce, D. (1982) 'The implications of greater openness for medical practice' (Unpublished paper presented to BAAF study day on 'Openness in AID').

Lawder, F. A. (1969) *A Follow-up Study of Adoptions: post-placement functioning of adoption families* (Child Welfare League of America).

Leeding, A. E. (1980a) *Child Care Manual for Social Workers* (Butterworths, 4th edn).

Leeding, A. E. (1980b) 'The local authority experience', in Hall, T. (ed.), *Access to Birth Records* (Association of British Adoption and Fostering Agencies).

MacIntyre, A. (1981) *After Virtue* (Duckworth).

Macleod, V. (1982) 'Whose child? The family in child care legislation and social work practice' (Study Commission on the Family, Occasional Paper no. 11).

McWhinnie, A. M. (1967) *Adopted Children: how they grow up* (Routledge & Kegan Paul).

Mandell, B. R. (1973) *Where are the Children?* (Lexington Books).

Manning, P. K. (1972) 'Locks and keys: an essay on privacy', in Heslin, J. (ed.), *Down to Earth Sociology* (New York, Free Press).

OPCS (1983) *Adoptions in England and Wales, 1981* (OPCS Monitor, FM3 83/1, HMSO).

Owens, D. (1982/3) 'Artificial insemination by donor: members' views', in *NACK* (National Association of the Childless, Winter).

Picton, C. (1982) 'Adoptees in search of origins', in *Adoption and Fostering*, vol. 6, no. 2.

Pincus, L. and Dare, C. (1978) *Secrets in the Family* (Faber & Faber).

Rautenan, E. (1976) 'Work with adopted adolescents and adults', in *The Search for Identity* (Association of British Adoption and Fostering Agencies).

Raynor, L. (1980) *The Adopted Child Comes of Age* (Allen & Unwin).

Rimmer, L. (1981) *Families in Focus* (Study Commission on the Family).

Rowe, J. (n.d.) 'The reality of the adoptive family', in *Child Adoption* (Association of British Adoption and Fostering Agencies).

Rowe, J. (1976) *Adoption in the 70's* (Association of British Adoption Agencies).

SCSRA (1968) 'Report to the Home Office on difficulties arising from the Adoption Act, 1958' (Standing Conference of Societies Registered for Adoption, April).

Seed, P. (1981) 'Fostering and adoption options in child placement policy', in *Research Highlights 1: Decision-making in child care* (Scottish Academic Press, Spring).

Selman, P. (1976) 'Patterns of adoption in England and Wales since 1959', in *Social Work Today*, vol. 7, no. 7, 24–6.

Shawyer, J. (1979) *Death by Adoption* (Cicada Press).

Smith, G. (1981) 'Discretionary decision-making in social work', in Adler, H. and Asquith, S. (eds), *Discretion and Welfare* (Heinemann).

Snowden, R. and Mitchell, G. D. (1981) *The Artificial Family* (Allen & Unwin).

Sorosky, A. D., Baran, A. and Pannor, R. (1978) *The Adoption Triangle: the effects of the sealed record on adoptees, birth parents and adoptive parents* (New York, Anchor Press).

Stone, F. J. (n.d.) 'Adoption and identity', in *Child Adoption* (Association of British Adoption and Fostering Agencies).

Strauss, A. L. (1977) *Mirrors and Masks: the search for identity* (Martin Robertson).

Stroud, J. (1983) 'Birth records: the next stage?, in *Adoption and Fostering*, vol. 7, no. 2.

Tizard, B. (1977) *Adoption: a second change* (Open Books).

Triseliotis, J. (1973) *In Search of Origins* (Routledge & Kegan Paul).

Triseliotis, J. (1976) 'Adoptees in search of their origins', in *The Search for Identity* (Association of British Adoption and Fostering Agencies).

Triseliotis, J. (1984, forthcoming) 'Obtaining birth certificates', in Bean, P. (ed.), (*untitled*) (Tavistock).

Walby, C. M. (1982) 'Adoption: a question of identity' (M.Sc. Thesis, unpublished, University of Wales).

Index